D0571354

The Essential Guide to
Shaping Children's Behaviour in the Early Years

RICHMOND UPON THAMES COLLEGE LIBRARY

RUTC

141755

The Essential Guide to Shaping Children's Behaviour in the Early Years

Lynn Cousins

Longman
is an imprint of

Harlow, England • London • New York • Boston • San Francisco • Toronto • Sydney • Singapore • Hong Kong
Tokyo • Seoul • Taipei • New Delhi • Cape Town • Madrid • Mexico City • Amsterdam • Munich • Paris • Milan

RICHMOND UPON ᴠIES COLLEGE
LIB H

141755 305·231(ou

PEARSON EDUCATION LIMITED

Edinburgh Gate
Harlow CM20 2JE
Tel: +44 (0)1279 623623
Fax: +44 (0)1279 431059
Website: www.pearsoned.co.uk

First published in Great Britain in 2010

© Pearson Education 2010

The right of Lynn Cousins to be identified as author of this work has been asserted by her in accordance with the Copyright, Designs and Patents Act 1988.

Pearson Education is not responsible for the content of third party internet sites.

ISBN: 978-1-4082-2502-8

British Library Cataloguing-in-Publication Data
A catalogue record for this book is available from the British Library

Library of Congress Cataloging-in-Publication Data
Cousins, Lynn.
 The essential guide to shaping children's behaviour in the early years / Lynn Cousins.
    p. cm.
 Includes bibliographical references and index.
 ISBN 978-1-4082-2502-8 (pbk.)
 1. Child development. 2. Child psychology. 3. Child welfare. I. Title.
 HQ772.C66 2010
 305.231--dc22
                                 2010001275

All rights reserved. No part of this publication may be reproduced, stored in a retrieval system, or transmitted in any form or by any means, electronic, mechanical, photocopying, recording or otherwise, without either the prior written permission of the publisher or a licence permitting restricted copying in the United Kingdom issued by the Copyright Licensing Agency Ltd, Saffron House, 6–10 Kirby Street, London EC1N 8TS. This book may not be lent, resold, hired out or otherwise disposed of by way of trade in any form of binding or cover other than that in which it is published, without the prior consent of the publisher.

We are grateful for permission to reproduce displayed references throughout the book from DfES (2007) *Practice Guidance for the Early Years Foundation Stage*. Crown Copyright material is reproduced with the permission of the Controller of HMSO and the Queen's printer for Scotland under the terms of the Click-Use Licence.

10 9 8 7 6 5 4 3 2 1
14 13 12 11 10

Typeset in 11/14 pt ITC Stone Sans by 30
Printed and bound in Great Britain by Ashford Colour Press, Gosport, Hants

The publisher's policy is to use paper manufactured from sustainable forests.

For Faye

Contents

About the author

Lynn Cousins has extensive experience as a teacher and head teacher. She has specialised in early years education and this formed the research area for her MA (Ed). As a special needs coordinator, a teacher in a special education school, a foster parent and a relief parent for children with complex needs, she has gained a wealth of experience in the educational and emotional needs of children. Lynn has written several books, contributed articles to educational publications and edited educational resources.

Acknowledgements

I would like to thank all of the children, at home and at school, who taught me so much about how people work and what children need from the adults who support them.

And thank you John for listening, for letting me bounce ideas off you on a regular basis and for all the cups of coffee that kept me going.

Introduction

In an ideal world children would all grow up to be happy, secure, confident and successful people. Given a loving and supportive environment this isn't impossible and children can realise these goals and become productive members of society. This society will be one which, as adults, they will help to shape so that it complements the values they will hold. And those values will be ones that you have helped to give them.

This process starts when children are encouraged to develop into sociable beings, as they learn how to behave in ways which conform to the patterns of behaviour that characterise the particular society to which they belong. Adults often describe this as behaving 'well' or 'being good'. As an adult you understand what that means without having to explain it further, but children don't necessarily know what it entails. One part of your role as an early years practitioner is to support the child as he develops the skills necessary to become that sociable person and to teach him what is acceptable in any place and at any time, and what is expected of him in different circumstances. This involves a long process of learning and development which starts on day one of life – or even before that.

Helping a child to find out about acceptable and pro-social behaviour can be described as *shaping* a child's behaviour. Every child will adopt a set of behaviours whatever happens to him; these could vary from deviant to acceptable to society. As you read this book you will find out that there are certain underlying, and apparently innate emotions which guide us all to behave in certain ways and it is in developing or modifying these that you can affect children's behaviour. It is vital to remember in all your dealings with the child that the quality and nature of a child's developing pattern of behaviour depends upon the people who surround that child, on their support and their responses to the child, his needs and his early attempts at socialisation. The family, naturally, has the greatest effect, but as a practitioner working in the care and education of young children you also play a major part as you interact with the child and his family.

In general, the young child doesn't decide to behave badly and annoy or upset others around him. His behaviour may sometimes be annoying or inappropriate. He can, and does, get it wrong. He can hurt and upset others – but there is nothing to be gained by simply blaming or punishing him. Rather, it is the way that the adults around him model behaviour, the way those adults treat the child and respond to him and the way they set boundaries and expectations (or not) that are the areas where any blame or praise for a young child's behaviour should be laid.

The behaviour of the adults in the setting is an enormous influence on the children's behaviour. Children model what they see, consciously and subconsciously, whether you intend them to or not! They will respond to your mood, your emotions and the way you express your feelings. They will notice how the adults around them interact with each other, as well as with different children. For these reasons it is important that you think about your own behaviour in the context of thinking about the children's behaviour.

> 'If school staff are to be able to help pupils develop social and emotional skills then they need these skills too.'

> (SEAL on www.standards.dscf.gove.uk/NationalStrategies)

This book explores both these aspects of behaviour within your setting, with each chapter having a focus on the adults' behaviour as well as the children's.

The book also examines many of the different ways in which the children will behave and suggests ways by which you can manage that behaviour, how you can encourage the positive and discourage the inappropriate. It is good to be able to base your responses on well-founded research and information, and for this reason you will find summary information from some of the influential names in the fields of child development and child psychology. Their theories have been used to suggest actions you can take as you interact with the children in your care.

Managing children's behaviour is seen by some practitioners as something that has to be done as an addition to fulfilling the requirements of the Early Years Foundation Stage (EYFS). This is a reactive approach. It is about waiting for the children to do something wrong or inappropriate and then responding to it with reprimands or punishment or even a behaviour programme.

Of course, it can feel challenging to find time to do everything and so it is easy to fall into the trap of not thinking about behaviour until it hits you in the face – maybe literally. This book tries to turn your thinking around, by managing children's behaviour as an integral part of the day's activities, as set out in the Personal, Social and Emotional aspect of the EYFS. Everything which is in that aspect of the EYFS can also be in your behaviour management policy. It can be part of your daily preparation and planning.

Managing behaviour and the Early Years Foundation Stage

The first aspect detailed in the Early Years Foundation Stage is that of Personal, Social and Emotional (PSE) Development. This positioning demonstrates its importance as it is the foundation on which all other learning is based. If this is not right then it is much more difficult for the children to learn. If you have to spend all of your time trying to make the children attend to you, then you are not going to find it easy to teach effectively. It is therefore important that you get this right.

The requirements set out in the guidance for PSE are:

> 'Children must be provided with experiences and support which will help them to develop a positive sense of themselves and of others; respect for others; social skills; and a positive disposition to learn. Providers must ensure support for children's emotional well-being to help them to know themselves and what they can do.'

(DfES, 2007, Practice Guidance, p 22)

'Experiences' and 'support' are both needed

'Experiences' have to be specifically planned by you. They are about teaching and learning. There are some parts of managing children's behaviour that are your direct responsibility. You have to be ready to actually teach children how to behave.

'Support', on the other hand, is about developing the children's skills and emotional capacities as they mature. It's about knowing your children and their capabilities at this time. Children's ability to manage their own behaviour depends to a certain amount on the age of the child, the level of his brain maturity, and what he is physically and emotionally able to deal with. Your role here is to be aware of the stages of the child's development and to respond in appropriate ways; it is about offering opportunities to use those developing skills, and to practise them in safe surroundings.

> 'Children's behaviour must be managed effectively and in a manner appropriate for their stage of development and particular individual needs.'

(DfES, 2007, Statutory Framework, p 28)

To help you to recognise these two aspects in your day-to-day management of the children's behaviour, Chapters 1–8 are clearly marked either 'Learn ...' or 'Develop ...'

Social skills

Chapter 1: Learn what is socially acceptable

The child learns that he is part of a larger group and how to enjoy belonging to it

Chapter 2: Learn what is morally acceptable

The child learns the difference between right and wrong

Respect for others

Chapter 3: Learn to respect other people, their culture and their property

The child learns that he needs to respond to other people, and the things that are important to them, in ways that will make those people feel valued, that this is a reciprocal act, and that he can expect to be valued in return

Chapter 4: Develop an ability to forge and maintain relationships

The child develops a sense of belonging to a group, and wanting to nurture that group

Emotional well-being

Chapter 5: Develop self-control and emotional balance

The child develops a growing ability to handle his own emotions and those of other children and adults around him

A positive sense of themselves and of others

Chapter 6: Develop self-esteem and personal pride

The child develops an awareness that he is special, that he has an important part to play

A positive disposition to learn

Chapter 7: Learn how to behave so that learning can take place

The child learns the skills that will help him to access learning; by doing this he will be behaving in the right way for these circumstances, that is, being part of an educational setting

Chapter 8: Develop a positive outlook on life

The child develops in confidence to the point where he can anticipate new challenges in life and in learning with excitement and pleasure, even if he is a little apprehensive

Chapter 9: Policy into practice

Bringing it all together: your policy, your practice and your professionalism

References to elements of the Personal Social and Emotional Development area of learning occur throughout the book.

Using this book

Use this book alongside your copy of the EYFS guidelines for Personal, Social and Emotional Development and your setting's behaviour policy so that you can relate them all to each other. These documents should fit together if you are taking a proactive approach towards your children's behaviour. The theories and practical ideas in the book may help you to deal with specific children or be an inspiration to you as you think about how you will be a force for good in these children's lives.

If you are in the process of re-evaluating your setting's behaviour policy look first at Appendix 1 on pages 205–213. This sample policy follows the main message of this book, which is that you are responsible for shaping children's behaviour, which is a much more positive approach than if you are merely considering how you will deal with any behaviour that your children present. The rationale for this approach, and details of how you can implement it, are the main focus of the book. As you read the book you will see how this all fits together. You may find that there are aspects of this that could be added to your existing policy, or it may suggest an alternative way of doing things in your setting.

The concept of a formal Code of Conduct for the adults in your setting may be a new one to you. There are some suggestions in Appendix 2, on pages 214–216, as well as ideas in each chapter of the book that would help you to create your own Code of Conduct. Alternatively, the ideas could form the basis for a professional development day, discussing how adults' behaviour can affect the children's behaviour patterns and how you can use this in a positive way in your setting. You may have decided not to have such a formal agreement, but the discussion and the heightened awareness of how the children learn from what they see and experience will be a useful tool in the management of behaviour in your setting.

Throughout the book you will find stories about Squirrel, who helps his friends and neighbours to behave as a community, supporting each other. You can use these stories with the children to explain or examine exactly what is meant by some of the rules of our society. There are more ideas for using these stories in Chapter 9, but this is where it starts.

Squirrel says

Squirrel lived at number 5 Warren Buildings, on the second floor of the tall block of flats. When he looked straight out of his sitting-room window he could see the rooftops and chimneys of the rows of houses on the other side of the busy road. But if he looked down, he could see a small square of grass, with a bench at one side, some climbing equipment and a red slide. And he could see the bays where the cars were parked. It was always busy, there was always something happening, always someone coming or going. Squirrel was never lonely up there in number 5. He looked out a lot and kept an eye on his neighbours.

Learn what is socially acceptable

What this chapter will explore:

- The nature of social groups in our society
- The importance of boundaries for keeping children safe and secure
- The need for rules and routines for children and staff
- How you can help your children to maintain the rules and routines
- How you can include the parents' views on safety

This chapter will concentrate on social conventions, by looking at why and how you will be setting boundaries and their importance to children's well-being, as well as creating rules and routines.

In order to work, society has to have some defining principles. These include the laws of the land, the rules of specific groups within the wider society and the accepted norms of behaviour, which are the social conventions by which you recognise your own community or society. One aspect of early education is to help your children learn what is expected of them as a member of society.

The child is born into the community of the family, recognising first the immediate family of parents and siblings and then the wider family of grandparents, aunts, uncles, etc. This social grouping has its own ways of behaving and its own traditions. Each member can be identified, they all know the way to behave when they are together, they laugh at the same 'in jokes', they all follow the same family traditions, such as the way that presents are distributed at Christmas. By conforming to its rules and conventions the baby becomes part of this community and starts to learn what these patterns of behaviour are.

Some social conventions may be culturally based. For example in western culture it is generally thought of as polite to look into someone's eyes when they are speaking to you. In some other cultures this is disrespectful, and you should avert your eyes, or look down when someone who is your superior is speaking to you. It is important to be aware that the conventions your children have at home may not be the ones you have in your setting.

When the children first arrive at your setting, each one will have a different concept of how to behave based on their own family and cultural experiences. In order to become part of this new community these children have to adapt their personal behaviours to a new norm. It will take time and patience to help the children sort out the acceptable way to behave here. Only then can they start to identify themselves as a coherent group with a shared set of conventions and traditions.

> **TOP TIP!**
>
> *Allow time during your initial meeting with new parents to find out about any cultural or religious conventions that the child will be expected to keep.*

Learning to be sociable

Children soon realise that different places and different communities of people have different rules and conventions.

- It's fine to run around and shriek when you are in the park. It's not fine when you are in the supermarket.
- It's fine to leave your toys on the floor in your bedroom. It's not fine to leave toys on the stairs.

● Mummy doesn't mind if you stand your cup on the table. Grandma likes you to use a mat underneath your cup.

The children have to learn the rules for the social environment that they are in and then remember which set of rules apply in their current situation. This involves much trial and error. The adults have to help them to remember what the rules will be or how they should be behaving in a particular setting, so that the children can behave appropriately.

Behaviour and Self-control: Planning and resources: 8–20 months

Share information with parents to create consistency between home and setting so that babies learn about boundaries.

Over time the children will learn to modify their behaviour to any situation and adapt it if that's necessary. For example: the children know that they can run when they are outside, but today a new little boy has started at the nursery. He is partially sighted and it will take him a little time to familiarise himself with the layout and resources in the outdoor area. The children will have to adapt their usual rule about running, 'We will all have to slow down and take extra care out-side so that we can watch out for Jamie as Jamie can't watch out for us.'

Adult support

It's not uncommon to hear adults tell children to 'behave' or 'be good'. These generic expressions imply that the children already know the rules and they are deliberately breaking those rules or ignoring them. With very young children, or in new situations, it may be that the child doesn't know or can't remember how he should be behaving. Asking children to 'behave when we get to the shop' isn't enough at the early stages of life. They need an adult to say to them, 'remember to stay next to me when we're in the shop' and 'hold on to the trolley when we get to the shop'.

Children need adults to recognise that they are trying to be socially acceptable, and that their intentions are good. What they need from the adults is a reliable reaction to guide them, so that they can learn to sort out behaviour that is desirable from what is undesirable. The response from the adult should always be directed at the behaviour and not at the child.

'It's good to see you lining up so well.' Not, 'You are all good children.'

'Pushing in isn't what we want to see. Please go to the end of the line.' Not, 'You naughty girl. Go to the end of the line.'

Reflecting on practice

Learning to stay safe

As part of their work on healthy eating, Emily, recently appointed as the nursery nurse for 'Ladybirds', was taking a group of children to the local market to look at and then buy some fruit for the fruit salad they were going to make. To get there they would be going along the High Street and then crossing the busy road to the marketplace.

Before they go she plans to remind the children about the rules of behaviour for when they are out of the nursery grounds.

She opens up a discussion with the children to raise potential dangers and risks and to encourage the children to think of the strategies to avoid them. These will be very important rules that must be followed.

> *'How will we get there?'*
>
> 'We'll go down the street and then cross over the road.'
>
> *'So what do we need to remember to do?'*
>
> 'Stay on the footpath.'
>
> 'Don't cross until you tell us it's safe.'
>
> 'Wait for the green man to come on.'
>
> 'Walk, don't run.'
>
> *'It's busy at the market. How will we make sure we don't get lost?'*
>
> 'Hold hands.'
>
> 'Don't go off with anyone else.'
>
> 'Stay near the teacher.'
>
> 'Stand still.'

Emily can now take the children out, reminding them of how to behave for each part of the journey or visit as they are needed. 'Remember to stay on the footpath' as they set off. 'Stand still and wait until I tell you to cross' at the crossing place. Or 'Stay close to me' when they reach the market.

This allows the children to start to think about risks and safe behaviours for themselves. They won't always remember or comply, but Emily can now remind the children in a firm but pleasant way instead of simply barking out orders for the children to follow in unthinking ways.

➔

> **Consider the following:**
>
> 1. By encouraging them to think about how to behave for particular situations, Emily is helping the children to take responsibility for their own safety. In doing this she is contributing to the important aim of learning to stay safe (*Every Child Matters*, www.dcsf.gov.uk).
> 2. Look for other opportunities like this to involve your children in discussing rules and strategies for keeping themselves safe.

Setting boundaries

> **Behaviour and Self-control: Planning and resources: 30–50 months**
>
> Set, explain and maintain clear, reasonable and consistent limits so that children can play and work feeling safe and secure.

Young children act in response to their emotions. If they feel angry, they hit out. If they feel happy, they giggle. They get cross because they can't do something, they kick and scream, or lie down on the floor and refuse to walk with you. How the adults respond to this behaviour can determine the child's future patterns of behaviour. The child needs to learn the limits of what society deems to be acceptable. They need you to tell them how far they can go – physically and metaphorically. Praising the behaviours that you want to see encourages the child to repeat them. Ignoring, distracting or admonishing the child for behaviour that you don't want to see should gradually reduce the repetition of this behaviour. If you ignore the child's responses – good or bad – the child will not learn that there are limits to what is acceptable and he will still be causing mayhem, racing round the supermarket with the trolley when he is ten years old.

Boundaries in this sense refer to the limits that you will impose. These limits may refer to the physical space, but they can equally well refer to acceptable behaviour, objects that can be handled or played with, or relationships between adults and children. Parents have been setting these boundaries throughout the child's life, and the boundaries have changed in response to the child's physical development and levels of understanding and self-control. Thinking about the objects for play or investigation it is easy to plot the changes that occur as the baby develops. The tiny baby may have a mobile to watch and reach out for, and is later offered a rattle or teething ring to hold. Soft toys with no sharp edges are available before moving on to building and stacking toys. Cupboard doors have to be secured as soon as the baby can move around independently, and then all the precious ornaments are placed on high shelves. And so it goes on.

Three criteria determine the boundaries you will set for the children in your care. Your aim is to create and work within boundaries that are:

1. Keeping the children physically safe.

2. Giving the children a sense of personal security.

3. Enabling play and learning to take place.

The first two criteria will be explored in this chapter and the third one will be the focus for Chapter 7.

Keeping the children physically safe: setting rules

Children's natural instinct is to explore, some will take risks and be into every-thing. Most children are fascinated by the world around them and want to know all about it. However, they are not automatically aware of the limits of their own abilities or the risks that exist in the world.

> *Self-confidence and Self-esteem: Effective practice: 16–26 months*
>
> Be aware of and alert to possible dangers, while recognising the importance of encouraging young children's sense of exploration and mastery.

As adults, aware of the dangers and vigilant for the child's well-being and safety, you will create boundaries for them. You create physical boundaries when you redirect them away from dangerous places and encourage them to investigate and test out those things you recognise as safe for them.

TOP TIP!

As you plan activities for the children you should remember that children are born explorers and investigators. They need to recognise those things that are dangerous, and learn to think about ways of using them safely, avoiding the dangerous aspect of something or working around the danger to minimise it. If children never face danger with the support and guidance of a caring, responsible adult they will be ill-equipped to live in the real world.

You shouldn't hesitate to provide things for the children to explore or things to test out, but you should always remember to remind the children of the safety factors as they start the activities:

'Always hold the closed blades of the scissors when you're handing them to someone.'

'Let's put all these beads back in the box so that they don't get on the floor. What might happen if we leave them on the floor?'

'We are going to crack open this egg to make our cakes. Wash your hands as soon as you have done that. Never put raw egg in your mouth'.

It's a good idea to make a note of potential risks and how you will help the children to respond safely to them, as you write your daily plans. Devise your own warning logo – an asterisk or a red exclamation mark – and put it next to the activity details so that you won't forget to mention safety procedures.

You may have to create some rules to keep your children safe because of the nature or limitations of the layout or environment of your setting. For example: if your outdoor area is L-shaped you will always have to have two adults available when children are out there, one for each 'leg' of the L. If you don't have the adults available at that moment, then the children have to come in or play in one designated part of the area.

There are other rules created to keep the children safe that the adults will be following but which will be unknown to the children. These are rules that are of extreme importance and as such will be maintained by all of the adults at all times. These include the rules about entering the building, identifying safe adults, locking medicines up or storing cleaning products out of reach.

Reflecting on practice

Pushing the boundaries

Children's urge to extend their world will mean that they will push the boundaries that you set for them.

Think about bedtime. A child needs rest and should have a regular routine and fixed bedtime. In certain circumstances, and as the child grows, the adults judge when to be flexible with the boundary of bedtime. The occasional late night is fine, when there is a party to go to, or visitors in the

→

home. But many children will try to push the boundary – 'five minutes more', 'please, mum' and tears are all tried.

Your job is to plan the boundaries, to help the children to relate to them, and then hold those boundaries firmly until you are sure the child is ready and able to go a little further. You can then extend the boundary.

Consider the following:

Are there boundary rules In your setting that mean children have to reach a certain age before they can use, for example, the longer slide or the higher climbing frame? Are you able to extend that boundary if you have a child who is particularly agile and adventurous and finds the small slide 'babyish'? Or can the timid child play a little longer on the small climbing frame where he has only just achieved success?

Giving the children a sense of personal security: creating routines

The early years of life are full of changes. As toddlers these children have already undergone many changes – as their physical dexterity and strength develop they can explore more of the world, they are becoming more independent in everyday tasks such as toileting and eating, they are starting to learn exciting new skills such as writing or counting. They meet many new people and have to learn different ways of behaving. They realise that they are separate beings independent of mummy and daddy, with their own choices to make. These changes, although exciting, can be quite unsettling to the young child and having a daily routine can be a source of comfort and reassurance.

Children brought up in homes where there are no boundaries can become very bossy and controlling. When their lives are unstructured they can come to feel insecure, unsafe and unloved. Their relationship with adults may be fraught with anxiety, because they won't know where they stand. In her book *Understanding Your 4 Year Old*, Lisa Miller describes the potential consequences when the adult doesn't maintain boundaries in a firm and consistent way.

> *'Simon has some idea that he is only small. He also has some idea that he needs looking after. If the big people in his life are to be under his control, behaving as though they can be bullied, who will be the people to take charge, and take care of him?'*

(Miller, 1992, p 32)

Routines act as a framework to the day; they give it a shape, they hold things firm. There are times for playing and times to sit together. There is a pattern to the session and children can anticipate the shared story time, or the time when they will have their snack. These daily routines make children feel secure and provide them with great comfort.

Why not try this?

Routines don't have to be boring

Try adding variety to your routines.

For example: everyday you have a story. The children sit with an adult and listen carefully. So how can you maintain this routine but also add variety?

'The story today is about a caterpillar – so we'll sit outside near some plants and hope a caterpillar might be listening with you.'

'The book today is about going to bed – so we'll all lie down, put the lights out and use a torch to light up the words and pictures in the book.'

'The story today is about a party – so we'll all wear the paper hats we made this morning.'

For some children a pre-school or school setting is the only routine that is stable in their lives and it offers them a chance to relax and to enjoy being a child in the care of supportive and supporting adults.

'Knowing what they can expect at various times during the day can make children feel more secure and in control.'

(Eisenberg et al., 1996, p 206)

The comfort/challenge balance

With firm boundaries in place and routines established, the children can be free to explore and develop. They can seek out experiences that are new to them, and test their own capacity for accepting challenges, safe within the boundaries you have created for them. Throughout their lives children will face change and make transitions, moving from one class to the next, one school to the next, or the moves away from home, to university, to making a home of their own. Life is full of these transitions. At this early age it is hugely important that the adults who are significant to the children, parents, care-givers and teachers alike, assist the child to experience transitions as positive moves. They may cause some apprehension – just think of the tension you feel as you start a new job – but they are also times of great excitement, of possibilities and opportunities. By providing a secure starting place with firm boundaries, and consistent, reliable adults, children can feel safe to test the water outside the boundary and accept new challenges in life. There is more about this in Chapter 8.

For some children transitions are a great trial. There are exceptional cases such as those children with difficulties on the autism spectrum who experience any change as a most traumatic event. The way that they can be handled can also be useful with any children who have a significant negative response to change.

Reflecting on practice

Ben, aged 4.6 years

Ben has been diagnosed as having Asperger's syndrome. He finds transitions very difficult. Any change of activity causes him great anxiety and distress, whether that is moving from playing to sitting at the table for his lunch, or getting up from the table afterwards to play outside.

The staff deal with this anxiety by preparing him for any change. As the time to change approaches they tell him, 'Ben you are going to sit at the table in five minutes time, to have your lunch.' One minute later, they tell him, 'Ben, you are going to sit at the table for your lunch in four minutes time.' They continue this countdown, minute by minute, until they can say, 'Ben you are coming to the table now to have your lunch.' They take him by the hand and lead him to the table. This has to be done consistently, and to the specific time mentioned. This becomes Ben's routine and with this level of preparation he learns to cope with the transition.

Consider the following:

Do you have any children who would benefit from this sort of support at times of change or transition – if only as a temporary measure?

At this age children are trying to come to terms with this exciting world around them. They want to know how things work, why things are as they are, what would happen if … They are trying to understand and make sense of their world. To help them, they need to know that this world is safe; it is the same today as yesterday and it will be the same again tomorrow. They need to feel that when they are tired from all the exploring they have done they can retreat within their personal comfort zone, where things are familiar, and they can sit quietly with their favourite toy, or hear a familiar story again.

Getting the children involved in rules

If rules are to be effective everyone must know about them and everyone should keep them. Everyone who doesn't keep them should expect consequences – even if that is just a gentle reminder. Your behaviour policy will indicate your boundaries and how you will manage them. You will be reinforcing your boundaries throughout the day and as part of your planned PSE work.

TOP TIP!

Use PSE or circle time to talk with the children about rules. Talk about the importance of everyone following the same rules in the same way.

What are rules?

When you talk to the children about rules, start the discussion by talking about some rules that they might be familiar with.

- What about the 'green man' at the crossing? What does this signal mean? What does the red light mean? What might happen if we broke this rule?

- Do the children know about driving on the left-hand side of the road? What would happen if some drivers decided not to keep to this rule? 'When we go abroad for our holidays we might have noticed that in many other countries they drive on the right-hand side of the road.' Point out to the children that what is important is that everyone follows the same rule.

Why not try this?

If your children are old enough you could try playing silly snakes and ladders. Two children play – but one of them is going up the ladders and down the snakes, whilst the other goes down the ladders and up the snakes. Do they think this is fair?

Talk about the rules in your setting

Behaviour and Self-control: Look, listen and note: 40–60+ months

Children's understanding of boundaries and behavioural expectations.

First of all find out from the children whether they know if there are rules in your setting. Can they tell you what they are? You will probably find that the children will tell you lots of negative rules:

Don't run indoors.

Don't hit anyone.

Don't throw sand.

Explain that these rules only tell you what you mustn't do, and ask if anyone knows what they should be doing instead. Work together with the children to turn their negative statements into positive ones:

Always walk when you are indoors.

Always be kind to other people.

Keep the sand inside the sand-tray.

Are there different rules indoors and outdoors? Be ready to prompt the children:

Is there a rule about the large climbing frame in the garden?

Does the water play outdoors have a different rule from the water play indoors?

Are there any rules about the weather when we go outdoors?

Are there any rules that are different if you are older or younger? For example: The blue slide is only for children aged three or under.

Encourage the children to think about why these age-related rules exist. Do they think they are fair?

Why not try this?

Social learning

Children learn a great deal by imitating those around them. When new children enter your setting what behaviour are they seeing? It's to be expected that the adults are setting a good example. What about the other children?

A useful expression to encourage your children to use is, 'We do it like this here.' When the new child heads towards the painting easel, another child might say, 'We always put aprons on when we paint.' When the new child wants to play outside when the rain has stopped, another child tells him, 'We put our wellies on here when the grass is wet.'

Remembering the rules

It is useful to start each term by talking about rules. It refreshes everyone's mind about them. It helps those who are new – adults and children – to learn about them. It is also important to consider how everyone remembers those rules. For the adults a list of rules can be compiled and displayed in a prominent place. For the children, it will depend on their ages and abilities.

Here are some ideas that you could try (further material for these ideas are available at www.pearsoned.co.uk/essentialguides).

● For resources or activities that have to be used by a limited number of children, laminate a card with the number on it – a numeric symbol and some spots or small pictures for counting. Place this near the activity.

● For resources that need an adult to be present make a card with a picture of a child holding an adult's hand.

● As general reminders of expected behaviour, divide a piece of card with a vertical line. On one side put a picture of unwanted behaviour at this activity with a cross or sad face. On the other side, a picture of the preferred behaviour with a tick or smiley face. Laminate it and fix it at the chosen activity, but where the children can see it – low down, at their eye level.

● If you have concerns about the children's behaviour in one activity – perhaps you have had a spate of sand throwing, or unacceptable quantities of water on the floor – you may decide to monitor the use of that resource. Have a white board near the activity, marked up as suggested above. This time, leave room under each symbol where you can write. Look at the children using the activity every ten minutes or so, and mark down the number of children behaving properly under the smiley face and those misbehaving under the sad face. Don't use names, just a tally mark.

At the end of the session show this to the children. Be pleased about all the well-behaved children's marks."I spotted ten children playing well, getting on with their tasks ...' And let them know that you were disappointed by the six sad faces marked on your board. Explain that they were doing things that you didn't want to see, and describe the behaviour. 'Now, tomorrow is our challenge. How many smiley faces can we get? Can we get more than ten? Can we get fewer sad faces? Can we get fewer than three?'

It is much more effective to use this as an opportunity to learn, and to show the children that you believe they can change their behaviour, rather than using it as a time to berate them and make them avoid this activity tomorrow.

TOP TIP!

Be positive when talking about rules.

Getting children involved in routines

Rules are broad images about behaviour management. They refer to the big picture. Routines, on the other hand, take those rules and make them specific to particular situations or activities. You could think of a map as an image of the rules; on it you can see your starting point and your eventual destination, as well as some of the pitfalls and high spots of interest that you could meet. If you now take a highlighter pen and mark the best route to follow to get to that destination, this is the equivalent of the role of routines.

Routines are particularly necessary for times of the day that involve a lot of change. It is at these times that you can easily lose control.

Making Relationships: Effective practice: 30–50 months

Establish routines with predictable sequences and events.

For example, when you are clearing away at the end of the session the children can be helping in their own way, but may well all be trying to do the same job, fighting over who gets to use the long-handled broom, or all avoiding the task of picking up the paper scraps underneath the cutting-out table! The rule may be that we all help to tidy up. But what does that mean, and how shall we organise it? This is where you need a routine that is known and adhered to by everyone.

Why not try this?

When do we apply routines?

Create a list of all the times in the day when transitions occur. These could be daily events or occasional activities. Think of all the times when adults or children are exchanging one activity for another.

You might include:

- Children arriving at the start of the session.
- Parents collecting children at the end of the session.
- Clearing up after a cooking activity.

For each of these, list the routines that are expected. Think of all the variations and try to cover them. You might have a list that looks like this:

Clearing up after a cooking activity

- Children place all the dirty equipment in the washing-up bowl on the table.
- An adult takes the washing-up bowl to the kitchen area and deals with it.
- Wipe the table.
- Sweep the floor.
- Wash your hands.
- Hang up your apron.

Once the adults have established the routines, you need to think of ways to teach these to the children. If your children can read then it is relatively simple to create some lists that you can display prominently and refer to, or point out to the children. 'We are going to tidy up in a few minutes time. Who remembers how we do that?' A quick reminder, pointing out the list, may be all that you need to do (see the companion website for further material at www.pearsoned.co.uk/essentialguides).

It is not so straightforward if the children are younger. For these children you may need to allocate tasks. Be sure to include the same tasks on each occasion so that the children come to expect certain jobs to be done. This is also a way to help the children familiarise themselves with the routine. The day may come when you can say 'tidy up' and they all know exactly what to do!

TOP TIP!

You could create a wall display of a routine such as 'tidying up', with paintings of children carrying out the various jobs – sweeping up, picking up toys, stacking things on the shelf, washing the table. This could then form your aide-memoire for the children. Choose a routine that you are specifically thinking about and include the discussion, the painting, the labelling, etc., as part of your PSE work one week.

Whatever approach you are able to take remember that this will be a slow, repetitive but ultimately worthwhile task.

'Children thrive on a regime which they can forecast.'

(Jenner, 1999, p 61)

Some of the benefits of having routines

The children will feel more secure when they know exactly what is expected of them. It is easy for times of transition to be an opportunity for some children to run wild. Others will find the time distressing. A routine is something to hold on to. When children know what is expected of them in very specific terms they will be more likely to behave calmly and keep busy in an ordered and structured way. The routine itself, and the activities it contains, helps them to see the way from the current activity to the next one, whether that is from leaving the care of the parent and accepting the care of the staff members, or from sitting quietly for a story to moving outdoors.

There will be less likelihood of routine tasks being overlooked. Once a routine has been established, it is much more likely that all the daily tasks will be completed efficiently and fairly. There isn't the chance for anyone to avoid clearing away thoroughly because the children will be wanting to know 'Who's sweeping up today?'

The time devoted to these routine tasks will be limited, freeing up more time for play and learning. When everyone takes over one of the tasks for tidying away, or arranging the chairs and tables for snack time, the job will get done in less time than if everyone is tripping up over the others trying to do the same job, while other necessary jobs remain untouched. If you have a routine that everyone follows you will need less time for these mundane tasks.

You will be able to find resources next time you look for them if they have been cleared away correctly. It is annoying when you find that the expensive piece of equipment you bought won't work because one piece is missing or damaged. The children also need to know that things should be looked after. We are conscious of living in a throw-away society, but society as a whole is beginning to realise that this is not a sustainable approach to life. Children have to learn that they should respect resources, that the resources are there for everyone and that they should always try to look after things and make sure that they are available for other children.

Children will learn that they have responsibilities as well as rights. The children will start to recognise that although they have a right to use all the resources available, they also have responsibility for looking after them. This includes tidying things away, stacking them carefully and making sure that all the parts are there. It is beneficial if children can access certain resources themselves. These will be kept at a level that the children can reach easily. If they are to have this right, they should also be expected to return items to the place where they found them, and that they should be in good order.

Dispositions and Attitudes: Effective practice: 30–50 months

Teach children to use and care for materials, and then trust them to do so independently.

Children enjoy having responsibility for small tasks, especially if they know that their hard work and commitment to completing the task given to them will be noticed, and they will feel proud of their achievement in finding all of the pieces of the farmyard puzzle, or clearing away all of the dressing-up clothes single-handedly.

Developing a professional Code of Conduct within the setting

Just like the children, adults need routines. They help us to manage our lives more effectively, both personally and professionally. Keeping to our routines helps us to become more organised. Being organised will help us to manage our time well, to make the most of every day, to achieve and to keep on top of things. This in turn is one way to reduce our stress levels.

Why not try this?

Building routines into your working day

Think about your working day. There are three areas that occur each day and which are fairly repetitive in nature and therefore lend themselves to a fixed routine.

1. Getting up and getting to work on time.
2. Setting up the activities for the children.
3. Keeping your records up to date.

For each of these devise a routine that suits you, your lifestyle and family needs and your personality. Some people prefer to be highly organised and will have a strict routine that rarely deviates. Others will need to have a degree of flexibility. Is there anything you could do to make your life less stressful at these times? If you're a night owl, packing your bag at night and putting your car keys on top of the bag could help you to leave home on time in the morning. Having an allocated space to store your paperwork may help you when you want to spend time planning or completing your records at home.

In addition to being organised as an individual, staff also need to be organised as a team, with everyone playing their part and taking their responsibilities seriously so that the whole team works well together. In your setting there may be some routines that you have to keep to in order to maintain the effective working of the whole team. It is good practice to review these routines occasionally to make sure that they are as effective as everyone thinks they are. By keeping to these routines you are setting a good example to the children as they see people cooperating, supporting each other and taking on their own responsibilities in an orderly and efficient way. In this way you are acting as a positive role model to the children.

In touch with parents – talking about safety rules

Parents are always concerned about their child's physical safety. They will want to know that you also take this seriously. One way to let them know this is to involve them in your thinking about rules linked to safety.

Behaviour and Self-control: Effective practice: 30–50 months

Share with parents the rationale of boundaries and expectations to maintain a joint approach.

Work as a staff team first, to identify any dangers. Think about safety under different headings. Try: indoor activities and resources, outdoor activities and resources, entry and exit procedures, visits and visitors, new children or staff members, toileting and hygiene, food and hygiene.

For each area that you choose, walk round that area, and think about the rules that you apply to maintain safety, and make a list of them.

You might end up with a list that looks something like this:

Climbing frame

● Only three children at a time may use it.

● It must only be used when an adult is present.

Sand

● No throwing sand.

● Adults will clean sand at the end of every session.

● Sand will be replaced every week.

Think about these rules as a team. Are they sufficient? Is there anything different that would be more effective? Make any changes and finalise your list.

Now circulate it to parents. In an accompanying letter explain to them that these are the rules that you are currently working by, but that you would welcome their opinions.

● What do they think? If they are not happy with anything they should suggest an alternative.

● Are there any areas that concern them that are not on your list?

● You might need to explain to them that there are certain regulations which are not up for debate, such as strategies for safeguarding children, vetting adults who work with the children, etc.

Take notice of their concerns and if you feel that they would benefit the children and improve the safety of your setting then amend your list of rules and circulate the new list to all parents.

TOP TIP!

Whenever you invite parents to complete a survey or questionnaire always report back to them with the final decision. Keep them informed and let them see that their ideas have been noted and/or used, or they may not bother to respond next time.

Conclusion

Society needs rules and routines if it is to function effectively and efficiently. There are different rules and routines that apply in different circumstances. Children need to have the chance to learn about these rules, and to practise following them within the safe boundary that you have set for them. Until children know what the rules are for any setting or activity, they can't be expected to follow them without a prompt or a gentle reminder from you. Whenever it is appropriate try to involve the children and their parents in the review or construction of routines for your setting.

Key ideas summary

You now have an understanding that you need to help the children to learn:

● How to be part of a social group.

● The rules and routines of the setting.

● The boundaries that keep them safe.

● That they have rights and responsibilities as members of a social group.

Going further

If you want to think about the rules and routines that will form part of your behaviour management policy, take a look at policies from other settings. You could try the Foundation Stage Forum. You will have to register before you can access this site.

www.foundation-stage.info

Squirrel says

Squirrel was about to go next door to deliver two birthday cards. One was a picture of a princess, the other was a racing car; and they each had a badge with a number four on it. Squirrel paused at the mirror in his hall twisting this way and that as he tried to check that his wonderful bushy tail was as sleek and smooth as he liked it to be. A noise outside on the landing made him stop. He moved nearer to the door and listened. It was Mrs Rabbit from number 6, the next door flat, calling out to her two children, Rose and Rowan.

'Don't go running off outside, you two. Wait for me at the door.'

The scampering feet and excited squeals outside Squirrel's door made him realise that the Rabbit twins were not listening to what their Mum said as they dashed towards the stairs.

Squirrel looked out of his window in time to see the two young rabbits appear, running out of the main door and straight across the car park towards the slide. At that very same moment Badger drove his delivery van – rather too quickly – round the corner. His brakes squealed as he saw the two rabbits. His van stopped just in time to avoid Rose and Rowan, but the white cardboard box that had been carefully balanced on the seat next to him didn't stop! It flew off the seat, its lid came off as it tumbled towards the floor and its contents landed upside down in a sticky heap in the dust. It was the birthday cake that Mrs Rabbit had ordered for the twin's birthday – and it was ruined.

Squirrel says,

'You should always do what the grown-ups tell you to do, especially near busy roads. They only want to keep you safe – and maybe your birthday cake as well!'

Learn what is morally acceptable

What this chapter will explore:

- What is meant by moral values
- How psychologists define moral development
- Whether you can teach moral values to young children and how you might do it
- How you can respond to children's moral (or amoral) behaviour
- Keeping parents aware of the moral values your setting upholds

This chapter will concentrate on what is meant by moral values, how they develop and how you can help children to operate within a moral code.

Behaviour and Self-control: Development matters: Early learning goal

Understand what is wrong, what is right and why.

Morals – what are they?

Thinking about morals could be described as thinking about what you ought to do. You may find it hard to explain why you do certain things or behave in particular ways. Sometimes you simply know 'what is right' or 'what is wrong'. Even young children seem to show an ability to discriminate in this automatic way.

This sense of morality is a much more intuitive feeling than the sense that you have to keep to social conventions. If you break a social convention no one actually suffers. When you break a moral convention then other people may be adversely affected.

Compare these two:

- It is the social convention in your office that you should wear a tie. If you don't wear a tie no one will actually get hurt.

- It is a moral convention that you should help someone in distress. If you don't call an ambulance for the old lady collapsed in the street there could be serious consequences for her health, even her life.

Moral development

A number of eminent psychologists have carried out research to discover how children develop a sense of right and wrong.

- As part of his psychoanalytic work, Freud looked at moral feelings.
- Developmental psychologists searched for a staged process of moral reasoning.
- Behaviourists set out to explain children's moral behaviour.

Some of their findings are summarised here to provide a starting point for thinking about the moral development of your children.

Freud

Freud claimed that someone's personality was composed of three parts, the id, the ego and the super-ego. The super-ego, which he says guides moral behaviour, has two parts – the conscience (which can cause you to feel guilty) and the ego-ideal (which contains the moral code that you hope to live by).

Freud also recognised that children learn much of their moral code from their parents, by imitating their behaviour.

Piaget

Piaget believed that children's ability to reason morally depended on their general thinking skills. As a developmental psychologist he divided up the stages of development through which children would pass. He called these:

The sensori-motor stage – birth to 2 years.

The pre-operational stage – 2 to 7 years.

The concrete operations stage – 7 to 11/12 years.

The formal operations stage – 11/12 years up to adolescence.

In line with these stages he saw the moral development of children as a staged process. Piaget saw children under the age of three or four years as being at a point when they don't understand the idea of rules; these children enjoy playing in ego-centric ways, that is, for their own pleasure and interest. He regarded this stage as being pre-moral. What he called moral reasoning started at about the ages of three to six years when children begin to abide by rules in an inflexible way, and believe that any action that breaks a rule will be met with punishment. At this stage, the consequence of any action is deemed to be the indicator of the seriousness of the action and thus of the level of the punishment that should be given – so if you break one cup, that is not as bad as if you break three cups. Not until children are about ten years old does Piaget believe that they understand that rules can be manipulated and that a person's intentions as well as their actions are to be taken into account.

Piaget's stages of moral reasoning

Pre-moral stage: under the age of 3 or 4 years

● doesn't understand rules.

Moral reasoning:

1. Heteronomous morality: 5/6 to 10 years (morality imposed from outside of yourself)
    ● begins to abide by rules in an inflexible way;
    ● believes that any action that breaks a rule will be punished;
    ● the consequence of any action is seen as the indicator of the level of punishment.

    →

---

2. Autonomous morality: 10 years onwards (morality imposed from within oneself)

- understands that rules can be manipulated;
- takes notice of intentions and circumstances.

Kohlberg

Kohlberg also thought in terms of cognitive development. His work builds on Piaget's work. He described six stages of moral development, which he grouped into three levels (two stages per level). His view was that every person goes through the stages in this order, and later research has backed this theory. However, not every person goes through all of the stages, and many people never reach the later levels even as adults.

Kohlberg's three levels are:

1. Pre-conventional.

2. Conventional.

3. Post-conventional.

Kohlberg's six stages of moral reasoning

Stage 1: concerned with outcomes and avoiding punishment.

Stage 2: follows rules that are of personal interest.

Stage 3: tries to win the approval of others in the family or small group they belong to.

Stage 4: rules should not be broken as that will bring punishment, and this includes the laws of the wider society.

Stage 5: the needs of the community at large may be more important than the needs of the individual.

Stage 6: consideration is given to the law versus conscience, and personal ethical principles develop.

Gilligan

Carol Gilligan asserts that boys and girls use different criteria on which to base their moral reasoning. This happens, she says, because of the different ways in which boys and girls are socialised. Boys tend to have justice and fairness as their central concern whereas girls base their moral reasoning on concepts of caring and responsibility.

Hoffman

Martin Hoffman believes that empathy precedes moral development. He describes five ways in which your sense of empathy may be triggered. The first three are involuntary, and Hoffman refers to these as primitive forms of empathy. They are:

1. Mimicry: a baby copies the facial expressions and movements of the mother, and this triggers feedback to the brain that then produces a feeling to match. From an early age the baby cries if he sees and hears another baby crying.

2. Conditioning: the baby, when he's being held, feels the physical effects of the mother's distress and is conditioned to respond to this. Eventually only the facial stimulus from any person is needed to trigger a response in the baby.

3. Direct association: when the young child notices someone in a situation that once caused them to feel distressed, they assume that the other person will be distressed in the same way.

The later two stages are under a person's voluntary control. Hoffman describes these as:

4. Verbally mediated association: language, written or spoken, can be the trigger that arouses feelings of empathy.

5. Perspective taking: from about the ages of two to three years Hoffman describes children as looking for clues as to how another person is feeling as they start to realise that others may feel differently from them.

The child may respond in one or more of these five ways at any one time.

Behaviourists

Behaviourists assert that children are influenced by the actions and reactions of parents and other significant adults. It is well known that children watch and copy the actions and responses of the adults around them. Research carried out by Zahn-Waxler and Radke-Yarrow (1982) found that the level of a mother's sympathy for others was echoed in the child's level of empathy towards others. What they see is what they do.

Other adult actions noted by behaviourists for affecting the way the child behaves include reinforcement by praise and the effect of punishment.

TOP TIP!

Remember that whatever the stage of the child's awareness of moral reasoning, it doesn't automatically follow that the child will always behave in a moral way. There can often be a gap between principles and actions.

Moral values

Moral values can be summed up in two main groups:

1. Justice.

2. Caring.

The first group of values is connected with the feeling that everyone should treat others fairly. These values could include justice, fairness, honesty, dependability, decency, equality, reasonableness, trustworthiness, integrity, fidelity, reliability and loyalty.

The second group of values arises from the automatic response to help when you see fear or hurt in other people. These values could include care, empathy, kindness, supportiveness, loving, sensitivity, responsiveness, consideration, understanding, appreciation, charity, patience, compassion, gentleness and affection.

The developing brain: responding to others

The part of the brain that is first to receive and respond to emotions is called the amygdala. This is set deep inside the brain, and in evolutionary terms it is one of the oldest parts of the human brain.

When you see fear or hurt in another person's face you automatically feel that you should stop what you're doing; that you shouldn't continue to do this thing which is clearly distressing someone else. This occurs because the amygdala is activated by the emotional stimulus of the pain or horror being expressed by the other person. It is thought that the close bond between a mother and her baby stimulates and maintains this normal function in the amygdala.

This empathy is what underpins the development of moral values, and thus, teaching children moral rules without also nurturing their emotional development will limit their capacity to respond appropriately.

Can moral values be taught?

Yes, but not in a void. Children need to see moral values in action within a context that is meaningful to them.

One way in which children at this young age are learning is through imitating adults. So this is going to be an effective route for teaching moral values, as children are encouraged to copy and practise moral behaviour.

> **TOP TIP!**
>
> *Children will start to recognise moral behaviour when you tell them about it when you see it occurring. Watch out for examples of kindness, fairness, justice and so on being shown by the children, or by members of staff, and comment on it in positive tones.*

How will they develop their own set of moral values? As they mature they will acquire greater verbal skills and thinking skills that are necessary to enter into debates about what is or isn't moral behaviour, but for now they will be relying on practising moral behaviour as a way to find out more about the values that are held by the society in which they live.

Learning to show moral values

You can provide young children with lots of opportunities to see how a moral code works in their own daily lives. You can make sure that they hear about the consequences of following or going against that moral code, and that they have a chance to copy the actions of the adults they trust.

> **TOP TIP!**
>
> *Spend some time to find opportunities within your planned activities when you can incorporate some direct moral value teaching.*

By thinking about some of the values from the list on page 26 you can examine how you can incorporate them into the daily life of your early years setting.

Fairness

'What can we do?' Take turns at a game or an activity so that everyone has a fair share of the fun and the learning

'Why should we do it?' Make time to explain to the children why they have to take turns by telling them about the consequences:

- If you take turns everyone has a go.

- If you don't take turns some children may miss out on their go and then they will feel sad, or upset.

> *Making Relationships: Look, listen and note: 40–60+ months*
>
> Children's acceptance that they may need to wait for something or to share things.

Consideration

'What can we do?'

- Tidy up, or leave activities neat and tidy, ready for the next person who would like to play.

- Pick up things when we've dropped them.

- Clean up when we spill something.

'Why should we do it?' Don't just tell children to tidy up. Explain to them why they need to do it and the effects of doing, or not doing it.

- When they tidy up after they have played with something it leaves the activity ready for the next child and this will make that child happy.

- Picking things up means that we keep our room safe so that someone doesn't fall over and hurt themselves.

- Mopping up means that we have a pleasant place to play in, not a dirty or sticky place. This makes everyone feel good.

- Helping to keep things tidy as the day goes on means that the adults don't have to spend ages at the end of the session putting everything away, and this makes them happy, and gives us time for an extra story.

> *Behaviour and Self-control: Look, listen and note: 30–50 months*
>
> How children show their care for others and their environment.

Reliability

'What can we do?' There are many small tasks that young children can take on. They can feed the fish, check that all the coats are on the hooks, hand out the snacks, and so on.

- Create a chart so that the children know what they are responsible for today (see an example at www.pearsoned.co.uk/essentialguides).
- Change it daily at the start of the session.

'Why should we do it?' The children will need to be told what it is they will do, and when they should do it.

- Explain that the fish are relying on the children to give them their food or they will be hungry.
- Explain about the need to look after their personal belongings and how this shows that they can be trusted to look after things that people give them – that makes the giver feel very happy, and glad that they gave us something.
- It makes us feel good inside when we do something that helps another person and giving out the snacks is one way of doing this.

At the end of the session the children can tell you all about what they did, and everyone can give them a clap for being helpful and responsible.

> *Making Relationships: Planning and resourcing: 40–60+ months*
>
> Involve children in agreeing codes of behaviour and taking responsibility for implementing them.

Gentleness

'What can we do?' Organise having a small animal or a baby visit you. The children can hold and stroke the animal, or play with the baby.

This is a super opportunity for children to show their quiet, caring side, particularly if you have children who are the youngest or only child, or those who may not be able to have pets at home.

It is a chance for them to practise gentle touches, quiet voices and calm behaviour.

Why should we do it? Explain to the children that when the visit takes place they will have to be calm, quiet and gentle, and the consequences of not doing this.

- If they rush around they will startle the animal and make it feel afraid.
- If they are calm the animal will begin to trust them and come near them, and may let them touch it.

- If they handle the animal they should do it gently so that the animal enjoys being stroked.

- If they are able to hold the baby they must be gentle so that they don't hurt the baby in any way.

- They must all be calm when moving around so that the baby doesn't get knocked over, which would make it cry.

- Quiet voices will help to keep things calm.

- Loud voices will startle animals and babies and make them nervous. They will be much happier in a calm, gentle atmosphere.

Reflecting on practice

Punishment or consequence?

The word 'punishment' has connotations of retribution, or deliberately wanting to hurt someone in order to teach them a lesson. This is never appropriate with young children.

A more suitable expression is 'consequence', so that children and adults alike think in terms of 'this action leads to this consequence'.

'If I push in, I will be made to go to the end of the line.'

'If I snatch that toy from someone I won't be able to play with it for the rest of the morning.'

Take notice of the vocabulary that is used by the adults in your setting when you see a child behaving inappropriately – and don't forget to include yourself in this! Try adapting it. Instead of saying 'If you do that you'll be in trouble', ask the child 'What will happen if you do that?' Encourage them to think about the consequences for themselves and for the other children.

Responding to behaviour

It is important for children's moral development that you respond to their behaviour when they demonstrate or neglect to follow a moral code of behaviour, whether they have been, for example, kind or unkind, fair to others or selfish, honest or dishonest.

TOP TIP!

Praising the behaviour that you want to see is reinforcing that behaviour, and reinforcement of any behaviour increases the chances of it being repeated.

Research has been carried out to examine the effect of praising pro-social, or moral, behaviour. One study showed that an effective approach, for the two-year-olds that were observed, was to talk to them about the consequences of their action – or inaction. Those children who were asked to think about the effects of their behaviour showed more empathy for others. Punishing, on the other hand, for not responding to someone else's need was viewed as unfair, 'But I didn't do anything' … exactly!

Behaviour and Self-control: Planning and resourcing: 40–60+ months

Affirm and praise positive behaviour, explaining that it makes children and adults feel happier.

But how you praise is important. The words that you use can help a child to understand their behaviour or else be meaningless sounds.

Reflecting on practice

Giving praise

Maisie is playing in the sand with her best friend, Sammi. They are focused on building a complicated castle, covered with tiny shells and shiny buttons. They have been concentrating on their work for a long time and it is nearing completion. As she presses a beautiful glittering button into the castle Sammi is accidentally knocked by a passing child, she presses too hard, and part of the castle wall, with its carefully decorated surface, collapses. Sammi is horrified, then upset, and starts to cry. Maisie puts her arm round her friend, and says that she'll help Sammi to build it again.

So what would you say to Maisie?

'Good girl, Maisie.'

'That's kind of you, Maisie.'

'I'm glad you didn't get cross, Maisie.'

'What a good friend you are, Maisie.'

➔

How will Maisie interpret your words? Will they help her to understand what it was that she did that you value?

Good girl: this tells her nothing. Was she good to build a castle in the sand? Was she good to hug her friend? This unfocused, almost throw-away statement won't develop her in any way.

That's kind: what was kind? Building, hugging, helping? What does she understand by 'kind'? Is it the same as your own interpretation of 'kind'? Why was it kind? You made a castle, you broke it and now you will build it again. Earlier this morning, Maisie made a jigsaw, broke it up, and then made it up again … was that kind? Nobody said so. A statement like this may help, but only if you know that she understands the word and its meaning, and if you add to it some explanation of what specific thing was 'kind'.

I'm glad you didn't … : so now, Maisie knows what she shouldn't do but does she know what she *should* do? She did a good thing, but that receives no adult attention. You are also putting ideas into her mind. She obviously hadn't considered getting cross, as the caring response she gave was instantaneous. There is no need to raise alternative strategies in instances like this. Don't draw attention to possible negative responses when there is a brilliant, positive response that could have been praised.

A good friend: this is a good start. Maisie's response may have been motivated by her love of her friend. Or this may be her natural response to anyone who shows distress. Take this a little further for maximum impact. Tell her what it was that you saw her do that displayed her thoughtfulness towards her friend. Tell her that offering support was a good thing. 'I'm sure Sammi felt better when you gave her a hug.' Let her know that offering to repair what was damaged was the best way to deal with a problem like this – helping to put it right and sort things out.

Consider the following:

1. How often do you comment on the good things that your children do?
2. Do you praise their good behaviour?
3. Do you explain what was good about what they did, and tell them why?

However, if a child is constantly misbehaving in a way that hurts or offends other people then you will have to consider some form of consequence.

Punishing alone has its limitations as an agent of changing behaviour in this context. Punishment doesn't help the child to understand exactly what he did that was wrong. Nor does it necessarily help him find out what he should do, or how he should respond in these circumstances.

An effective approach is to explain what he did (or said), describe to him the consequences of what he did, how the other person feels now, what he could do to make amends and what he should do in these circumstances in the future. And then add a consequence of your own that reflects what he did and that is immediate. Whenever possible, involve the child in this as a discussion so that they start to take some responsibility for their own actions.

Reflecting on practice

Responding to children who hurt or offend others

Think first:

- Is he old enough to be aware of the consequences of his actions?
- Does he know the alternatives?

Find out:

- Whether the act was intentional.
- Did he mean to hurt?
- Could it have been avoided?
- Was he provoked?
- Is he under any stress at the moment? This may provide a reason, but not an excuse. It is something that you should take into consideration when you deal with him.

Match your response to the child, the incident and the frequency of such incidents:

- Talk through the whole event with the child, reminding him exactly what he did.
- Talk about the effects on the other person.
- Talk about how everyone feels about this.
- Discuss possible alternative strategies – include the child in this discussion, don't dictate.

If the act was intentional, you may decide to impose a consequence:

- Tell the child what that consequence will be and why that particular response has been chosen. Make sure it fits the incident – 'There is only time for one more go on the slide for everyone because it's nearly lunch-time. You will have to wait until last to have your turn as you have been pushing in and that's not fair on the other children who missed out on their turns.'

→

- Above all, carry this out as soon as the incident occurs. It is of no value if you wait. The child needs to experience the adult's displeasure when he is feeling the anxiety that will accompany any intentional wrongdoing.

If it wasn't intentional, then it's not appropriate to impose any consequence:

- Helping the child to find an alternative way to behave would be the more effective route to improving his moral behaviour.

Consider the following:

1. Look again at the sanctions outlined in your setting's behaviour policy with this approach in mind.

2. Do you need to make any changes to your current methods to make them more helpful for developing children's personal value systems?

Developing a professional Code of Conduct within the setting

Morality could be described as a set of rules that help you to know how you ought to behave. The standards that you expect of yourself are a manifestation of the level of your moral development. Looking back at Kohlberg's theory (p 24) you will find that at stage five there are people who have the needs of their community at heart. They recognise that there are times when the community's needs must override the individual's needs. This is a good principle by which to guide your professional interactions.

Everyone in the community is of equal importance. Everyone deserves the same level of respect, or kindness or care. So at the heart of your Code of Conduct should be a sense of equality.

The people you work with will all have different levels of responsibility, different roles to play and different needs to be met, but fundamentally everyone deserves to receive the same level of respect. Whatever a person's gender, family, ethnicity, physical or mental abilities – you should treat them all with the same level of respect, honesty, kindness and so on. Your moral values should remain the same.

If the children are to move towards this level of moral development, where they are to recognise the needs of the community – however far away that stage must seem at this point – they need to witness adults working and interacting in this way. So in your Code of Conduct there may be a general statement about the attitudes that you will take to other people, and a requirement that you maintain these attitudes with equality.

Responding to lapses of moral behaviour within the setting

Elliot Turiel (1998) has researched the development of children's moral reasoning. His 'domain theory' is based on his proposition that children organise rules into two domains: morality and social convention. He states that they see social conventions as negotiable whereas they see moral rules as ones that can never be broken or altered, even by people in authority. Turiel has found that children from about four years of age can distinguish between these two sets of rules. If this is the case you have to consider carefully how you attend to children's behaviour.

If children understand that social convention has a set of rules that are negotiable, they may view the breaking of these rules as fair play. If moral rules are never negotiable then they will expect a consistent response from adults in authority on the occasions when these rules are broken. In order that these responses are applied consistently by all of the adults who work with the children, they should form part of your agreed behaviour policy.

Why not try this?

It is worth spending time as a staff team to examine:

- how you respond to lapses in moral behaviour;
- whether everyone takes the same approach;
- the effectiveness of your current approach;
- whether everyone is applying the rules consistently;
- whether there is anything that could be improved upon;
- whether there is anything that needs changing straight away.

Your responses can be an intervention to stop the behaviour on any particular occasion or an intervention to teach the children about alternative ways of behaving. Each has its place, and there will be times when you have to do both of these, especially if someone is being hurt.

TOP TIP!

The children's individual circumstances, the quality of their home life, their age and abilities should always be taken into account when you intervene in disputes.

Some common moral lapses that you may meet with young children are:

● telling lies;

● name calling;

● taking other people's toys or personal property;

● spoiling other children's work.

Take some time to look at these lapses, considering why they may occur. Armed with that knowledge you can discuss with colleagues how you might respond. Here are some ideas that you may want to think about.

Telling lies – not being honest

Sometimes children tell lies because they are afraid to tell the truth. If punishment at home is harsh for even accidental breakages or injuries, the child will be programmed to cover up. At all costs he wants to avoid a punishment. If this is the case it will take a long time and many occasions when you will have to respond in a fair and just way, until he realises that he can own up when he has done something wrong.

Sometimes the lie is so obvious that you can reply with a firm, kind, 'Er, I don't think so. Do you?' and a twinkle in your eye. This suits the occasion when Charlie is covered in red paint and tells you that he hasn't done any painting yet, or when Grace tells you that she didn't cut her hair even though she has scissors in one hand and a tuft of blonde hair in the other.

Some lies are told by children who want to impress you, or who want their world and their experiences to be better than they seem to be. These children may have low self-esteem and you need to respond by praising their efforts, giving lots of attention to any kind or thoughtful gestures they make. Make a point of telling the others about good things they have done, and telling the parents about their hard work, concentration, politeness – anything that gives them praise where it is due. There is more about this in Chapter 6.

TOP TIP!

Praise honesty. When children tell you about something they have broken or spilt, or that they hurt Ben when they ran into him, deal with it in a calm way. Praise the child for letting you know that something needed sorting out, fixing or clearing up, or that someone needed first aid. Let the children see that in this sort of circumstance there is no need to lie. Just deal with the problem, involving the children if possible, and then carry on with what you were doing.

Name calling – not being sensitive

This can range from comments about someone's appearance to racist abuse. For the victim it is highly offensive and degrading; it can become a form of bullying with all its ramifications. It is essential that this is not ignored, however mild or amusing it may seem at an early stage. There is more about bullying in Chapter 4.

Children can have strong feelings about the names they are called – even the 'pet names' that families may use. Coming into a new environment may be a chance for them to use their real name. Ask children what they like to be called, and stick with it.

Why not try this?

- Talk with the children about names and their importance.
- What name might they give to the fish in your tank, a new puppy, or a new baby brother or sister?
- Think about names from different countries.
- Investigate some different kinds of naming ceremonies as a way of introducing the children to the idea of the importance of our names.
- Names are so important that we write them with a capital letter!

You can now talk about the fact that it is hurtful when we call people names or when we mock their appearance or name. Encourage the children to think about what it must feel like, how sad or upset they might be. Whenever it occurs, make sure that you pick up on it, that the child is reminded of how hurtful it was, and that an apology should be given.

Behaviour and Self-control: Look, listen and note: 40–60+ months

Children's awareness of the consequences of their words and actions.

Taking other people's toys or personal property – not being trustworthy

This is a situation that most definitely needs a response that is in line with the child's developmental stage.

The child doesn't have a sense of self until he is about 18 months old. Before this self-awareness is established he can't be motivated by the idea of possessing something. If he takes something from another child then it is more likely that he just wants to play with it, that he has seen the other child exploring something and he wants to explore it as well (Licht et al., 2008). At this stage you can probably offer the first child an alternative toy, and peace will return.

Once the child is self-aware he may take toys in order to provoke another child, just to see the effect he can have on someone. He may be trying to assert his own rights, by holding a toy that he doesn't actually want to play with – but simply so that he can exert power over another child. In these situations you should take steps to demonstrate that each child has rights.

'Tom had the toy first. He is playing with it. When he has finished playing with it he will give it to you if you ask nicely.'

'You can have the next turn. Tom can play with this for five more minutes and then he will hand it to you' – but make sure that you remember to prompt Tom when the five minutes is up.

'The toy belongs to everyone. You have had a long turn. In two minutes it will be Ellie's turn and you will give it to her then.'

Behaviour and Self-control: Planning and resourcing: 16–26 months

Duplicate materials and resources to reduce conflict, for example have two tricycles or two copies of the same book.

Some children will have a favourite toy and get upset if someone else plays with it. This child may be feeling insecure. Over time you can work with the child to deal with this, but while it is still a problem you may have to allow the child to 'have' this toy and provide a special place where it is kept. It may be that the child is an only child who has no experience of sharing. Again, this will be a long-term response, explaining why they have to share, and encouraging the child to find alternative activities.

Some children will simply like the look of something and decide to have it. They may take it home, with or without the adults' knowledge. Use a PSE session or Circle Time to talk about the fact that if everyone takes home the toys they like there will soon be none left here – and then what will you do all day?!

TOP TIP!

It is probably worth having an amnesty every now and again, when children and parents can discreetly bring toys back and put them in a 'returns' box.

Spoiling other children's work – not being considerate

The accidental knocking over of someone's tower of bricks is just one of those things that happens in a space full of energetic children. Children have to appreciate that the fact it was an accident doesn't preclude the child from being upset when his hard work is damaged. Children need to think about the hurt that this caused and that perhaps they need to slow down or look where they are going. The child who is upset needs help to see that it was just an accident and that they can build it again. A friendly act of support from the one who knocked it over may be welcome.

Sometimes children choose to deface someone's work, scribbling over a picture or tearing up a painting. This child needs to face the outcome of his action. He needs to see the child who is upset. He needs to know that the adults are not happy. But he also needs someone to find out why he did it. Was it a case of low self-esteem? Does he damage another child's work because he recognises it as being better than his own, and he wants to stop them getting the praise? Is he getting enough praise and attention for his efforts, even if the outcome isn't always very good? Is he jealous of a particular child? This child needs to have some positive attention once the immediate situation has been dealt with. Only then will he stop this behaviour. For more ideas on dealing with this, see Robert's case study in Chapter 6.

In touch with parents – about your setting's moral code

Moral values tend to be universal and the general assumption is that everyone else lives by the same moral code that you do. It is still worth taking the time to write down the values that you hold as a staff team and the way you expect them to be shown within your setting. This could be part of your setting's brochure or prospectus. It should certainly be made known to the children's parents.

Why not try this?

What are our moral values?

Look again at the list of moral values on page 26. Decide, as a team, which ones best describe your setting's values.

Now choose two or three from each list. For each one decide how you would expect to see it in action, how you would recognise it or what behaviour the adults or children might be engaged in.

→

For example:

- Consideration – children will say 'excuse me', 'please' and 'thank you'.
- Patience – adults will allow time for children to think through what they want to say, and not interrupt them.

These statements could be in your brochure. They could become the focus of some of your PSE work. You could decide to write to parents about one of them in your newsletter, involving them in the children's development of moral behaviour.

In your newsletter you could write to parents:

- explaining how you are concentrating on some particular aspect of moral development;
- describing how you are encouraging this aspect;
- informing them how good the children are at behaving in this way;
- asking for parental help by expecting this behaviour at home;
- thanking parents for their support in encouraging this behaviour in the home.

You could talk about moral development in a parents' meeting.

Adapt the staff activity, above, and engage the parents in discussion of how people carry out the moral values that they claim to hold – or not.

Encourage the parents to join in a discussion such as: 'What do we do in our everyday life which shows that we follow a moral code?'

Applying this to their children will help all parents to consider the need for respect and fairness in all their interactions.

Conclusion

In this society a sense of morality, based on issues of justice and caring, underpins the way life is lived and all of the expected interactions between people. You are now aware of the importance of recognising these moral values when you see them in action in your setting, and of drawing the children's attention to this. It is also part of your responsibility to the children to model a moral code in your dealings with your colleagues, parents, professionals and the children themselves. In this practical way children will begin to understand the moral values that they too should be showing.

Key ideas summary

You now have an understanding that you need to help the children to learn:

- That everyone follows a moral code.

- How they can behave within this moral code.

- What will happen if they break that moral code.

- That you will recognise and praise them when they keep to that moral code.

Going further

A useful debate on the subject of values is the report for The Children's Society, *A Good Childhood* (Layard and Dunn, 2009). This goes beyond education, but has informative discussion on the society and family circumstances of the children you will be working with.

To find out more about how the brain works there are two books that provide excellent starting places.

For physiological information, try:

Carter, R. (2003) *Mapping the Mind*, London: Phoenix.

To find out more about the impact of early experiences on the development of the brain try:

Gerhardt, S. (2004) *Why Love Matters. How Affection Shapes a Baby's Brain*, Hove: Brunner-Routledge.

Squirrel says

Squirrel had just made himself a cup of tea in his finest china cup and saucer, the one with the gold edges. He carried it carefully across the room and was just setting it down on the table, next to his brown leather chair, when a dreadful squeal from outside startled him. Squirrel tutted as the tea slopped into the saucer. He went to the window to see what was going on. →

The squeal had come from Frankie Ferret. He was standing near the slide, his hands in his pockets, his head down and his feet shuffling as the other five Ferret children played football on the grass. Squirrel opened his window and called out to the children.

'What's wrong with Frankie?'

The eldest Ferret, a girl called Fran, who was in goal, replied:

'He's cross 'cos he can't be in goal.'

'Why can't he be in goal?' asked Squirrel.

''He's too little. He lets all the goals in!'

'Well surely you could let him have a turn for a few minutes.'

'We-ell.'

'It would be a kind and friendly thing to do. And who knows, he may get better at it.'

'Oh, okay. Come on Frankie. Seeing as you've stopped squealing, come and be the goalie – but it's only for a little while, and then I'm going back in goal.'

Squirrel says,

'It's good to let every one have a turn, even if they are smaller than you or not as good at something.'

Learn to respect other people, their culture and their property

What this chapter will explore:

- How children develop opinions about other people
- How children view other people
- How each child needs respect as a unique individual
- How all children deserve respect in equal measure

This chapter is all about how the child learns that he has to respond to other people, their property and the things that they value in ways that will make those people feel valued. He must also learn that this is a reciprocal act, and that in return other people will value him, his property and the things that he values.

Showing respect is about finding a way to treat all people the same, at the same time as recognising and valuing the things that make them different. It is a balance between seeing each child as unique and seeing each child as an equal with all the others. Getting this balance right is not an easy task. The behaviour that you use is a signal to the children about the behaviour that they should use when they interact with others, and as they learn how to treat other people. The child's level of maturity, their capacity for making judgements and the stage of their brain development means that these young children rely on copying what the important adults around them are doing as they start to judge other people, and give or not give respect.

Learning to judge other people

The new-born baby accepts anyone who picks him up or responds to his needs without discrimination, whether that person is his mother or a complete stranger. It isn't until they reach about seven months that babies begin to show signs of anxiety when meeting new people. They look at the mother's face, and sense her reaction in an attempt to find out whether this is a person that they should trust. This is known as 'social referencing'. Even the toddler, once he can get around independently, regularly returns to the mother or main care-giver for reassurance. If you watch carefully you will notice that the child moves away to explore his surroundings, and then returns to the mother to touch her, or be picked up by her. Then just as quickly he is happy to go off exploring again.

> *Making Relationships: Look, listen and note, 30–50 months*
>
> Children's strategies for coping with change.

This way of judging people may still be the way that some of your children are operating, but now they are using you as the point of social reference. They may be looking at you to gauge your reaction when they are faced with a new situation.

TOP TIP!

Your response could trigger a chain of reactions with far-reaching consequences as the child mimics the emotional response he sees you give. If you can look positive then this will reassure the child. If you look anxious, or grimace and back away, then their anxiety will be increased.

One type of occasion to be ready for is when you have a visitor in your setting – perhaps the dentist is in talking to the children about cleaning their teeth, or you may have a clown entertaining everyone as part of your work on the circus. For some children this will be a time of anxiety and you may notice them watching you. Think carefully about your own reactions.

Reflecting on practice

Danny, aged 4.7 years

Danny was visiting his new school for the first time. His mum thought he wouldn't want to go, so she hadn't told him about it. They went out one afternoon and there they were – at the school. Danny's mum had found school difficult. She had struggled with her reading and couldn't wait to be old enough to leave.

When they entered this new place, Danny looked up at his mum. He saw the fear in her eyes, felt her palms sweating as she clung on to him. He held back when the teacher approached him. He hid behind his mum when it was suggested that he should 'come and play with our toys'.

Danny wouldn't be starting school for another few weeks yet. During that time he frequently asked his mum if he *had* to go. The night before, he cried and wouldn't stay in his bed.

Consider the following:

1. If you were the teacher and were faced with this situation what could you do to help Danny and his mum as he starts at your school?
2. If you were the EYP at Danny's pre-school what could you do to help prevent similar situations arising? You will be preparing the children for moving on to school – can you also prepare the parents?

Developing opinions about people

Children are still learning about society and the way that it's organised, and they are taking clues from you – these may be verbal or non-verbal. Of course you are entitled to have your own personal opinion, but it's your professional duty to show no discrimination at all in the workplace.

> *'Young children readily disregard what adults say if they observe them doing otherwise.'*

> (Fancourt, 2000, p 124)

Society isn't perfect but if children are to learn to respect people then they must first learn that all people deserve respect in equal measure. Some of the areas where discrimination could happen are connected with gender, culture, class, age, physical ability, sexuality and status.

> ### Sense of Community: Effective practice: 16–26 months
>
> Be positive about differences and support children's acceptance of difference. Be aware that negative attitudes towards difference are learned from examples the children witness.

Encouraging diversity

Set some time aside to carry out an inventory of your resources. (See www. pearsoned.co.uk/essentialguides for an example audit sheet.) Do you show a fair mix of gender, culture, age and physical ability? Check your:

pictures and posters;

story books;

dolls;

house play equipment;

food (toy and real);

dressing-up clothes;

volunteer helpers;

staff.

Next time you are ordering new resources look again at this and try to include different people and cultures if you can.

> ### Dispositions and Attitudes: Planning and resourcing: 16–26 months
>
> Ensure resources reflect the diversity of children and adults within and beyond the setting.

Why not try this?

Ways that you can treat all the children with equal respect

- Expect every child to help with the tidying away: wiping tables, collecting up toys, etc., finding a suitable role for everyone.

- Create tasks that everyone can do, or adapt activities so that every child can access them.

- Sometimes set the role-play area out with male-dominated jobs such as a garage, a workshop, a building site, and encourage girls as well as boys to play there.

- Be careful in the way that you respond to children. Do you encourage boys to 'be brave' when they hurt themselves more often than you might say this to a girl? Do you accept behaviour in boys that you wouldn't accept from girls? Do you excuse difficulties? 'It's because he's a boy' or 'Girls are rubbish at …'

- Provide role-play outfits suitable for boys and girls, e.g. white coats for doctors (who could be boys or girls), white jackets for male nurses or females if they're wearing trousers.

- Have dolls and their clothes from a variety of cultures – not just the ones represented by your children.

- If you are doing some work about a festival that is new to you, seek advice from members of that community. Don't do all your research from books – they may be misrepresenting things or giving a stereotypical view.

- Hold a celebration day when you experience the food, clothes, dance and art of another culture.

- Include books in mother tongues for any children who have English as an additional language, so that their parents can read with them.

- Include a variety of foods and recipes when you cook with the children. Ask for help if you're not sure how to prepare something.

- Invite grandparents as well as parents in to help with some activities.

- If you are doing some work on the family, make sure that you include all the variations your children are part of.

- Arrange for your letters home, and leaflets, etc. to be available in all the languages spoken in your setting.

You need to employ a little lateral thinking when you are setting up the activities for the children. Set up an obstacle race that the children go around on their bikes, so that they understand what it is like to be in a wheelchair having to negotiate busy pavements. Borrow some 'feely' puzzles as used by children with visual impairments.

| Reflecting on practice |

Tea, anyone?

The foundation stage class staff had noticed that the boys rarely played in the role-play area. With a professional development focus on equal opportunities for all children they made a plan. The role-play area was set up as a workshop. There was a counter to which children could bring their broken toys and equipment. There were blank cards, pencils and an old diary available to create a system for recording who had brought what in, and what was wrong with it. There was a work area with tools and a selection of 'parts', as well as some old watches, clocks, radios, etc. There was a kettle and a couple of mugs for the workers.

On the first day Carol, the teacher who had set it all up, found three girls in there, sitting by the kettle making tea and chatting!

There were no boys in sight.

Consider the following:

1. Did the children know what to play?
2. Had they ever seen a workshop?
3. Did they know how the system works?
4. What lessons could Carol learn from this?
5. Think of some ways in which Carol could address the problem and get the most from this good idea for role play.

Self-confidence and Self-esteem: Planning and resourcing: 30–50 months

Provide role-play areas with a variety of resources reflecting diversity.

The developing brain: relating to others

About 40 per cent of the cortex of the brain consists of the frontal lobes, which are situated just behind the eyes. This part of the brain has evolved very quickly – in evolutionary terms – and accounts for the fact that the human brain is comparatively much larger than the brains in other species. However, this is one part of the brain that develops, almost entirely, after birth. There is a period of increased development in early childhood and a further burst during puberty. It may not fully mature until adulthood.

It is described as the part of the brain that gives us free will. It enables us to plan for the future, to choose how we react. It is responsible for our ability to control our thoughts, emotions and actions, make judgments and organise our lives.

So, with this delayed development very young children can't be expected to understand social niceties, or to do things simply to please other people. If you are doing your best to feed the baby, and the baby doesn't want that food, then no matter what you do he's not going to eat it. He has no concept of eating something because that will make *you* happy!

If this part of the brain is to develop it has to be nurtured. The experiences the baby has will affect how it develops, and will create a brain that suits the culture and environment that the baby is part of. Social relationships are an important factor in this development and the baby needs to have lots of happy, loving contact.

It is thought that there is a critical window for this development. Children brought up in extreme deprivation don't develop this social skill, even when their circumstances are changed. You may remember the tragic stories of children in Romanian orphanages. They were never able to benefit from those missing early social experiences even when they were given to them later in life.

Theory of mind

If children are to be encouraged to respect the beliefs of other people they first of all have to have an understanding that these other people have beliefs and that they may not be the same beliefs as their own. The ability to do this rests on the child having a theory of mind.

The mind has numerous facets. In your mind you know things, feel things, desire things, believe things, think things. You know that other people can do similar things in their minds. You also know that they may feel differently from how you feel, think differently, know different things, hold different beliefs. This awareness of the fact that other people have other feelings, or beliefs, and may interpret things in a different way is, in a nutshell, having a theory of mind.

A great deal of work has been done to find out when children develop a theory of mind. Some researchers have suggested that the complexity of the language involved in the tasks can affect the findings as it may be that the children didn't fully understand, or couldn't explain themselves adequately.

Research that supports the development of a theory of mind

Many psychologists have studied this over many years. Their theories and their research findings are contained in many books about child psychology (two important texts being Schaffer (2004) and Smith et al. (2003), whose ideas are outlined below). This is just a short summing up of some of the findings.

Flavell (2002): between the ages of three and five years children's understanding of the mind changes considerably.

Language. Bartsch and Wellman (1995): from about two years onwards children use words such as 'want', 'wish' and 'like'. From three years they start to use words such as 'think', 'know', 'remember' and 'wonder'.

False belief: this indicates the way that children make assumptions about other people's behaviour. It shows that children are able to construct their own representation of the world in their mind. Under four years old children work on the principle that other people see the world as they do, that everyone has constructed the same representation. So they believe that everyone else knows what they know. At about the age of four this changes. Children under the age of four years don't understand that someone else can hold a belief that is different from theirs. If they know the facts they assume everyone knows those same facts. This means that three year olds don't use false belief to deceive someone else. By the age of five they can do this.

At three years:

> I know that there is only one biscuit left in the red tin.
> I know that Mary wants a biscuit.
> Mary asks me where the biscuits are kept.
> I tell her – in the red tin.
> She takes the last biscuit and eats it.
> I don't have a biscuit!

At five years:

> I know that there is only one biscuit left in the red tin.
> I know that Mary wants a biscuit.
> Mary asks me where the biscuit is.
> I tell her – in the blue tin.
> Mary looks in the blue tin
> There are no biscuits in it.
> She goes away.
> I have a biscuit!

→

Despite the outcome, three year olds continued to tell the truth when a test similar to this was repeated. They assume that Mary knows where the biscuit is already, because they know that fact.

Five year olds know that others can hold different beliefs from theirs and so they tell Mary a false piece of information, realising that it's possible for her to believe that.

The Sally–Ann test: this is used by psychologists as the way to find out whether children have developed a theory of mind.

> Sally has a basket.
> Ann has a box.
> Sally puts a marble in her basket then goes away, leaving the basket behind.
> Ann takes the marble out of the basket and puts it in her box.
> Sally returns and wants to play with the marble. Where will she look for it?

Under-threes reply 'In the box', because they know where the marble is, and therefore assume that Sally knows what they know.

Four year olds reply 'In the basket', because they understand that Sally doesn't know what they know. She has a false belief.

Seeing and knowing: By the age of three years children know that something exists even if they can't see it and that if they hide something other people can't see it. They know that someone else may be seeing something different from what they are seeing (the different picture on the other side of a card, for example). They also know that other people may not know something that they know. By four years of age they know that other people may see things from a different angle (to me it is right way up, to you, across the table from me, it is upside down)

Representation: Children can recognise a picture of an apple as an apple. They know that toy food is not the same as real food. What they have more difficulty in understanding is when something is represented in an unusual way. (Imagine those party games where you have to identify a picture of something from an unusual angle.) In their play they may use a pretend object to represent the real thing. They might also use the toy version to represent another object altogether: toy banana for a real banana; toy banana for a telephone. Children will play along with a friend's representation. If one child talks into the banana/phone, then hands it to a friend to 'say hello to granny', the second child will go along with the representation.

Respecting individuality

The Early Years Foundation Stage refers to 'the unique child', reflecting the fact that every child is a competent learner in their own way. There is also an expectation that practitioners will promote diversity and difference. When children leave the small setting of the home and become part of a larger group it is easy to be 'lost'. Children may feel that they are just one of the crowd here, whereas at home they have a distinct place and role.

This could lead to two particular behaviours, neither of which have positive benefits.

1. The first is that the child's self-esteem could suffer. There is more about this in Chapter 6, but it is also worth linking this with the concept of respect. By respecting the individuality of the child you are supporting their self-esteem.

2. The second is that the child may use the cover of the large group to indulge in behaviours that he wouldn't get away with if he was in a one-to-one situation with an adult. When you show him that you respect him, you let him know that you know all about him, that he has a special place here in this setting, that you welcome his individuality, and that you most definitely know all that he is doing.

Why not try this?

Using names

Of course there are occasions when you will use generic words — everyone, children, yellow group — but it is also worth looking for opportunities when you can refer to the children by name.

'Ben, can you get the box to put all the cars in? Ask Tom, Sarah and Jo to help you to collect them all up.'

Rather than:

'Can the children playing on the car mat put everything away now.'

If you want a group of children to come and work with you ask for one of them by name.

'Josh. It's your turn to come and do some writing with me.'

When he arrives give him Anna's book.

'Could you find Anna, please, and ask her to come and join us.'

→

When Anna arrives, give her Sol's book ... and so on until you have your group.

As each one finishes he can take the book off to the next child that you want. This is a practical way for the children to learn the names of the others in their group.

Sense of Community: Effective practice: 16–26 months

Help children to learn each other's names, for example through songs and rhymes.

Activities to promote difference and diversity

Sense of Community: Development matters: 16–26 months

Learn that they have similarities and differences which connect them to, and distinguish them from, others.

Read *Elmer* by David McKee

This will be a familiar story to many children but still has a good message of what it is like to be different. Act out the story. Ask the child being Elmer,

'What does it feel like to be different?'

'Do you like being different?'

Let as many children as possible have a turn at being Elmer.

Try the following website link to access a template of Elmer which the children can colour in using the fill tool on a simple art programme: www.naturegrid.org.uk/infant/earlyict. You want the 'Senses' section of this link.

Musical groups

Everyone dances around until the music stops (or you stop playing the tambourine or drum if you want to do this outside). You call out a group type and everyone who fits that group sits in one designated place, and everyone else sits in the other place. You could use two sides of the room, two benches or two adults as the markers for the two sets of children.

Try:

> everyone with brown hair;
>
> everyone with black shoes;
>
> everyone wearing something red;
>
> everyone who likes oranges;
>
> everyone who has a brother;
>
> and the occasional everyone who has two ears – just to prove that in some ways we are all the same.

TOP TIP!

This is a good strategy for sending children to get their PE bags, or outdoor coats to save a crush. All children sit on the carpet with you. Send out: 'all those with short socks', 'all those with buttons' and, for the final few, 'all those with noses'.

Soft toy medley

Collect together some soft toy animals or dolls.

You will need to have several that are the same in some distinctive way, and one that is different. For example, several in the same colour (different shades of one colour is fine) and one in a different colour, several with four legs and one with two, a collection of teddies and a doll or several with happy faces and one with a sad face.

Ask the children, 'What do you notice about these friends?' Once they have identified the similarities and the difference engage them in a discussion:

> 'Has this one got a smile? What is making him happy?'
>
> 'Why is this one sad?'
>
> 'Do the others let this one play?'
>
> 'Can he join in with them?'
>
> 'What can he do that the others can't do?' (Be creative: He can ride his bike without stabilisers. He can fasten his own shoes.)

You want to work the discussion round so that the children start to see the positive side of being different, and recognise that in some way everyone is different. Everyone is unique.

'Imagine what it would be like if we were all exactly the same. How would you find your Mummy at the end of the day when she comes to collect you? How would your Mummy know it was you? It's really good that we are all different in some ways.'

Being special

Sit in a circle and you start by saying,

'Everyone is special in their own way. What makes you special?'

'I'm special because I can *run very fast.'* Or some other skill you have.

The children take it in turns to speak,

'I'm special because I can write my name.'

'I'm special because I can whistle.'

Don't force those who are shy, just carry on with the next person in the circle.

On another occasion let each child say why someone else is special. It may be one of their friends in the group. It may be someone at home.

'My dad is special because he can play the drums.'

'My gran is special because she buys me sweets.'

'Ravi is special because he can climb to the top of the climbing frame really quickly.'

Equality for all

Recognising differences means that you can then plan for equality. Ways must be found to enable every child to have an equal opportunity to achieve, and to do their best.

Considering physical needs

How you help children to achieve all that they can will depend on their physical needs and their capacity to learn. You may have to differentiate the level of practical help that you give, the way in which you encourage individual children, or provide additional help or time, or different resources. So in these practical ways you will be treating children differently, in the search for equality. It is an effective way to model showing respect.

Reflecting on practice

Stuart, aged 4.9 years

Stuart started school using a wheelchair. The classroom was fully carpeted and he found it difficult to manoeuvre his chair in the crowded room. He preferred to get around the room on his bottom or crawling, and as many activities were at floor level he felt quite comfortable with this. To reach his personal belongings he was allocated a drawer at the bottom of the cupboard.

Stuart, aged 5.4 years

Stuart has progressed to using a walking frame indoors. He can get around the classroom at speed. His drawer is now kept at the top of the cupboard so that he doesn't have to reach down to get his belongings.

This is a simple change but it makes a lot of difference for this little boy. It allows him to be independent and therefore the same as all the other children.

Consider the following:

Whenever you are about to receive a child with physical limitations spend some time looking around the room and thinking about how he will get around, access all the activities and reach the resources that the others can reach.

Rewarding behaviour

The behaviour of some children means that you have to implement special programmes for them. They may seem to be getting extra attention or rewards for behaviour that the others show all the time. How can you prevent the other children from viewing this as injustice? The fact is that all children need you to notice that they are doing good things. They need you to reinforce appropriate behaviour that complies with your rules and routines. This is necessary for their self-esteem at all stages of life. As an adult it is still great to have someone praise your efforts and notice what you have done. For young children it is additionally important as they are still learning what is meant by 'being good'.

> *Self-confidence and Self-esteem: Effective practice: 40–60+ months*
>
> Explain carefully why some children may need extra help or support for some things, or why some children feel upset by a particular thing. This helps children to understand that when it is required their individual needs will be met.

Catch them being good

Have you ever listed all of the things the children do that could be termed 'good' behaviour? It's surprising how long that list could be. Here is a sample of what might be on your list. It could go on and on …

Behaviour that we want to see

- Hanging their coat on the right peg.
- Bringing their book back.
- Having their indoor shoes with them.
- Putting their name up for self-registration.
- Sitting quietly at the snack table.
- Putting their name on their painting.
- Remembering to ask an adult to put their name on their paper before they paint on it.
- Wearing an apron at the water-tray.
- Mopping the floor when they spill water.
- Waiting patiently for their turn on the slide.
- Helping their friend up when he fell over.
- Putting their cup away after their drink.
- Getting to the toilet in time.
- Washing their hands.
- Turning the tap off.
- Putting waste paper in the bin.
- Saying please and thank you.

All of these are worth rewarding with some acknowledgement from you. It might be:

- a smile;
- a thumbs-up sign;
- a word of praise: 'Sam, well done', 'Jenny, thank you'. (Always say the name first so that the child knows it's him – or her – that you're referring to. If you say it afterwards s/he may have missed the praise before s/he listened!)

If you take this approach then all of the children will be receiving praise for their behaviour throughout the day. The children will accept that some children get their praise in a different way. The danger lies when some children tidy away and their efforts go unrewarded, while another child has lashings of praise and public ovation for doing the same thing. As you will remember from Chapter 2, children have a great sense of fairness and justice. They like to see this in action. So everyone needs to be praised for the action, even though that praise may take different forms. In doing this you are showing respect to the children for the efforts they are making to behave.

Reflecting on practice

Nicky, aged 3.4 years

Nicky's older sister, Daisy, has severe cerebral palsy. She is confined to a wheelchair. Whenever it comes to tidying toys away Nicky refuses to help, screams and runs off. Nicky's mum couldn't get Nicky to cooperate despite all the different approaches she'd tried. Nicky just didn't want to know. His attitude was 'Daisy doesn't have to. Why should I?'

On his first day at nursery Nimisha, his key worker, asks everyone to help with the tidying up. Everyone does so – except Nicky. He continues to play for a while, and then goes and sits at the table for his snack. Requests to come and help are totally ignored.

After a few days of this behaviour, Nimisha tries a new plan. She tells Nicky at the start of the session that he is in charge of the farm set today. He must set it out and he must put it away safely at the end of the session. She helps him with these two tasks, as a supporter, letting him take the lead.

During Circle Time Nimisha asks the children what they can do for themselves. They suggest 'I can put my jumper on by myself', 'I can wash my hands without my mummy helping 'cos I can reach the taps now', 'I can put my cereal in my bowl at breakfast time' and so on.

They discussed the way that they are all starting to be able to do more things, and that they can do things for themselves now that they used to need help with. They are growing up. 'Let's give ourselves a clap for growing up!' Nimisha explained to the children that showing that you can do all of these things – dressing yourself, feeding yourself, looking after your toys, putting your things way – is how the adults know that the children are growing up.

Consider the following:

1. Nimisha showed that she understood Nicky's problem. She knew enough about his family circumstances to recognise how this situation had

→

arisen, and to know that simply insisting on him joining in with the tidying up wasn't going to work.

2. She approached the problem from a totally non-judgemental way. She did things to help Nicky learn what is expected, and to recognise his achievements in terms of growing up.

3. She was able to tell Nicky's mum of the approach she had tried. Nicky has started to tidy up along with the other children at nursery. It will probably take a little longer to change his behaviour at home.

4. Is there anything you think Nimisha could talk about with Nicky's mum to help her?

Self-care: Development matters: 22–36 months

Seek to do things for themselves, knowing that an adult is close by, ready to support and help if needed.

Caring about their environment

Behaviour and Self-control: Development matters: 40–60+ months

Consider the consequences of their words and actions for themselves and others.

This can stretch as far as you are prepared to take the idea of 'the environment'. It could include:

respecting other people's property;

respecting the nursery or classroom resources;

respecting the world.

All of these depend on the behaviour that arises from:

● understanding the concept of ownership, whether that is to one person, or to a group of people, or to humankind as a whole;

● having an insight that some things are replaceable, some things are finite, other things have a sentimental value which is more than the price;

- being willing to take care of all things because you have a sense of empathy with other people.

The concept of ownership

Once a child can understand that he is a separate person he can start to learn about ownership of possessions. This is usually at around 18 months.

Name labels above coat hooks, names on work, a special place to keep your PE clothes, are all simple ways to show the child that he has a special place to keep the things that are his. This is his place. It encourages a sense of ownership and a respect for personal belongings.

Chapter 2 has some ideas for dealing with children who take other children's toys on pages 37–38.

Why not try this?

Toys from home

What to do with toys that the children bring from home is an issue faced by most settings.

Children may bring a special toy or old blanket that is a comfort to them when they are tired, stressed or unwell. Deal with this sensitively. The toy is very important to the child, but he needs to know that it is you, and the other important adults in his life, who keep his world safe. If the toy isn't there you will still make sure that he is safe. You may want to consider having a cut-off point for these. Perhaps:

- An age-limit: now you are ... you should leave it at home, give it to mummy to take home with her or put it in the special basket.
- When you have just started at school, you may bring it in for one week, and after that it must stay at home or in the special basket.

Make a special basket to leave out as children arrive. This should look attractive, but be removed to a safe place during work and playtime. It should be brought back into view at the end of the session when the children are preparing to go home.

Make a point in your prospectus and in your induction talks with parents about these expectations, and about the fact that it is their responsibility if they choose to leave it in the basket, rather than take it home.

If a child regularly brings some huge toy you will need to have a word with the parents and encourage them to replace it with something more practical. Everything should fit in the basket – you can't be storing lots of huge stuffed animals. →

Children may bring in a new toy to show the others when it is their birthday or granny has brought them a toy koala back from her trip to Australia. Encourage the children to talk about their toy to the group at Circle Time. Then it goes on to a high shelf, where they can see it but not reach it. Explain that this will keep it safe from paint or glue, or getting lost.

The concept of value

When children have many possessions, or when they are frequently bought new toys or the latest gadgets it is easy for them to think that things can be, and will be, replaced. Conversely, if children think that breaking anything is going to result in severe punishment they may decide that it is preferable to lie or hide the pieces. Somewhere between these two extremes is a place that lets children see that they should look after things, but that accidents happen, things wear out, and that this is natural, and acceptable.

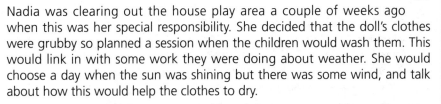

Reflecting on practice

New toys for old

Nadia was clearing out the house play area a couple of weeks ago when this was her special responsibility. She decided that the doll's clothes were grubby so planned a session when the children would wash them. This would link in with some work they were doing about weather. She would choose a day when the sun was shining but there was some wind, and talk about how this would help the clothes to dry.

The day arrived and the children were enjoying the soapy water. Some of the clothes were quite old and well used and when they were washed holes appeared in the seams, and the fabric came apart in some places. Nadia told the children that it wasn't worth continuing to wash these pieces. She explained that they had been used a lot and were now worn out and not fit for use any more. She gave them to Josh to put in the bin.

They had a system in place where several parents and grandparents made clothes for the dolls on a regular basis, other parents bringing in balls of wool or offcuts of fabric for them to use. There were usually some new clothes in store. Together with the children, Nadia looked through and some replacement pieces were chosen.

The next day, Michael and Annie were in the house. An argument broke out over who should have the new jacket for the teddy. Both children hung on to it, both children pulled hard – and the sleeve came away. 'We'd better throw it out and get a new one out of the box,' suggested Josh.

Consider the following:

If you were Nadia how would you respond?

1. How would you explain the difference between things wearing out and damage arising from anger?

2. Should these two children ask one of the grans to mend the jacket, along with apologising?

In your own setting:

1. Do you include the children in your clear-out sessions?

2. Do they know why you sometimes throw things away, or when you decide to buy new resources?

3. How do you let the children know about new resources?

TOP TIP!

Have a box or crate for resources that are damaged in some way. Make a label showing a sad face with an over-sized tear drop made from silver foil.

Once a week empty the box with the children. Count the number of things in the box. For every item in the box put on a sadder and sadder face and body posture. Decide together – can it be fixed, and how and by whom? Is it of no more use? Was this an accident? We can replace it. Was it anger or carelessness? We will have to wait until we have some spare money to replace it. What a shame, we shall miss using it.

If there's nothing in the box – celebrate!

Being green

Childhood is a time for setting standards of behaviour. One of these that can easily become part of the norm for the children is to think about ways they can respect the planet. You can:

- have separate bins for paper, plastic and food waste;

- grow vegetables in part of your garden area or in large planters in your playground;

- create good habits about turning off taps, not wasting water and paper towels, and not leaving lights on when there is no one in the room.

This doesn't have to be a flag-waving, eco-warrior approach. It should just be normal practice that will have a side effect of saving you money.

Behaviour and Self-control: Planning and resourcing: 30–50 months

Collaborate with the children in creating explicit rules for the care of the environment.

Developing a professional Code of Conduct within the setting

One way in which you can show respect is to maintain confidentiality. This is a major issue when you are caring for children; there are no shades of grey here, no stretching of the boundaries. Nothing short of perfect behaviour is acceptable.

Personal information

You will be privy to a lot of personal information given by the parents on their admission forms: details of their address, their contact numbers, their marital status, where they work, etc., as well as a child's achievements, medical conditions or areas of difficulty. Some families will have contact with other agencies such as social care or the police. This information is often only shared on a 'need-to-know' basis. When you are trusted with this sort of information, then live up to the trust that has been placed in you. Be careful about what you say about any of this, who you say it to, and where you are when you say it. You don't know who might be related to whom. You don't know who might be listening in. You don't know who has a grudge over another family.

Compare this with the information that you have to give when you apply for a job, or the notes made during your interview or appraisal. You wouldn't want to think about it being discussed with strangers over a drink. The same applies to parents and children. They deserve the same level of respect for their personal information as you do.

What do you do when there are volunteers present?

The manager should be telling them about confidentiality, just as she told you. They should maintain the same standards as you do.

Be a good model. If they ask you for information – tell them that you can't discuss those sorts of details with them. Let them see confidentiality in action. If they are parents themselves they should appreciate this, and the way that staff in your setting respect parents' and children's business will soon be public knowledge.

TOP TIP!

Children also need to learn how to identify those people who are not safe. We have to talk with them about respecting their own internal feelings. Rules about not going off with strangers have to be broached as children reach the age when they may play outside with their friends. There are programmes available, and training for staff should be in place. Find out about this when you take on a new job.

Explain to the children that you use ways to keep them safe in the setting. You may have an intercom system on the door, video surveillance cameras and identity badges for welcome strangers. Whatever your system – point it out to the children when you are dealing with this subject.

(Every Child Matters: Learning to stay safe, www.dcsf.gov.uk)

In touch with parents – at the end of the day

Building a partnership with parents clearly rests on the ability to build a relationship with them. Parents have to trust you with their child. You have to merit their respect by the professional and caring way in which they see you responding to their child's needs. Parents may be anxious about leaving their child. Some may be feeling guilty that they have to go to work when they would like to be at home with their child, others may feel guilty at having some 'me time' away from a demanding child – and enjoying it. So the time when they collect their children at the end of a session can be one that is quite emotional. This may be shown or it may be hidden.

It is also a time of great emotion for the child. The anxious child may be overwhelmed with relief that mummy didn't forget them. Others may be desperate to show off their work or tell about their day. Some will be tired and will welcome the thought of going home.

Imagine what it is like, in the midst of all that emotion, when the teacher or key worker approaches you, with the child in tow, to tell you about some misdeed.

- It is very easy for the parent to overreact, to feel obliged to 'do something'.

- The child will wonder why the issue is being raised again. Was it not sufficient for you to deal with it?

- Unspoken questions could then arise. Should the children respect you next time you have cause to check their behaviour? Is your word not enough? Is it only when the parent intervenes that the child's behaviour can be adequately addressed?

Reflecting on practice

Respecting parents feelings

'At the induction meeting with parents we talk about the end of the session, when the parents will be reunited with their child. We tell the parents that when they arrive to collect their child we will tell them about what has been happening for their child that day.

'We will tell them about milestones that have been reached, or whether he ate all of his lunch, if the parents are anxious about such things. We will tell them about accidents or health concerns. Anything that is relevant to that child on that day. If the child has done something wrong at some point, and we have had to speak to them about their behaviour or their language, for example, we will let the parents know what occurred and what we did about it.

'The need for the parent to feel informed about the events of the day and of how we managed their child's behaviour is important in working together in a real partnership of care. It may in fact prepare them should we need to take the next step of putting a behaviour plan in place. It also ensures that parents are aware of our expectations and positive approach to behaviour management.

'We then emphasise the fact that we are not expecting the parent to get cross about it with the child – we have already dealt with the issue and moved on. What we would appreciate is for the parent to talk about the incident at some later point, especially if it's a recurring problem. We would like them to tell the child that 'when you did/said that you made Faye sad'. Their verbal support and positive input is so important in achieving positive results.

'But we stress that this should be a matter for later, not when they are meeting up at the end of the session. We remind them that the end of the session should be a happy time when parents and children are reunited. We make sure that children each have something to show the parent. There should be a happy atmosphere between them at this special moment.'

(Faye, manager, Halstead Pre-school)

→

Consider the following:

1. What do you do to make sure that parents and child meet up in a positive way?

2. How do you manage the sometimes necessary business of telling a parent something unpleasant?

3. Do you think the child should be present when you give the parents information about some incident in which they were involved?

Conclusion

Respecting other people depends on you recognising the worth of those other people, and what makes them special. Children have to be able to recognise the ways in which people are all different in some way as well as noticing the things they have in common. It is initially through watching and copying you that they will start to learn how to treat other people with dignity and respect.

> 'Find opportunities to give encouragement to children, with practitioners acting as role models who value differences and take account of different needs and expectations.'

> (DfES, 2007, Practice Guidance, p 22)

Your role is to be fair to all of the children so that everyone has the chance to achieve as much as they can and to be as happy as they can be. Respecting the children means that you will be finding ways to allow this to happen.

Key ideas summary

You now have an understanding that you need to help the children to learn:

- That everyone is special and that it is good to be yourself.

- That everyone deserves the same respect, whatever their age, gender, family or role.

- That other people may think differently from them.

- That they should respect their environment.

- That other people should show respect to them.

Going further

Find details of the specific duties that schools have under the Race Relations (Amendment) Act 2000 by going to:

www.equalityhumanrights.com

Follow the link to 'for organisations' and then put *'Sectoral guidance: schools'* in the search engine on that page.

Independent nurseries and pre-schools are not obliged to follow the procedures but are urged to do so 'as the arrangements will help them to promote good race relations'.

Squirrel says

Squirrel had a really sore throat and he'd decided to have a day at home, resting. He made himself a hot drink and was sipping it carefully as he sat in his chair watching all that went on outside Warren Buildings.

He saw Ramsay Rabbit riding about on his new, silver bike; the one that he got for his birthday last week.

He saw Ramsay jump off the bike and leave it at the side of the bench before dashing up the stairs back home for something. Squirrel wondered what that might be.

He saw Herbie Hedgehog coming down the path, his lips pursed as if he was whistling. He saw Herbie stop at the bike, and look around, and then he saw him getting on to the bike and riding off on it.

He saw Ramsay come back, go to the bench, stop, look. Ramsay's hands went up in the air and he squealed. His mum came out. Squirrel saw her face – she looked very cross with Ramsay, she was pointing her finger at him. Ramsay was crying. They both went indoors. Perhaps they were going to phone the police!

Squirrel saw Herbie riding back towards the building. He stopped at the bench, jumped off the bike and put it back where he had found it. He had only wanted a ride. But it would have been much better if he'd waited and asked Ramsay if he could have a turn. Squirrel went to phone the Rabbits to let them know that the bike had been returned.

Squirrel says,

'Always ask if you want to borrow something. Don't just take things that don't belong to you.'

Develop an ability to forge and maintain relationships

What this chapter will explore:

- Understanding how children form attachments
- Helping children to make friends
- Helping children to understand the requirements of friendship

This chapter explores how you can help a child to feel that he belongs to the group and how he can contribute to the group. To do this he has to be able to relate to others.

As the children are learning about respect for other people you can be helping them to develop their ability to make friends. This is a practical way to introduce them to the idea that they are part of a larger group. The mechanisms of giving and taking, of tolerance and acceptance are basic to friendship as well as to membership of any larger group.

Developing attachment

From birth the baby relates to other people. Although this may be indiscriminate in the first weeks of life, the baby soon learns to recognise the person who is most often present giving care and security. It is with this person that the baby forms an attachment.

Attachment theory

'Attachment' here simply means 'relationship'. The attachment that a child has with his mother, or other main care-giver, sets the pattern for the way he will deal with other relationships throughout his life.

Much research has been carried out on children aged 12–14 months, using 'The Strange Situation' (Ainsworth et al., 1978), which concludes that there are four main types of attachment. One of these is a secure attachment, the other three are insecure attachments:

> *Secure*: these children use the mother as a base from which to explore, are distressed when the mother leaves them, and greet the mother in a positive way when she returns.
>
> *Avoidant*: these children don't mind being left with a stranger; they avoid contact with the mother.
>
> *Resistant*: these children are distressed by separation from the mother; they seek comfort but also resist that comfort when she returns.
>
> *Ambivalent or disorganised*: these children have no method for dealing with stress, they seek the mother out but also avoid her, and show contradictory responses to the mother.

Most children fall into the first category and are securely attached to their mother, which means that they are able to form new relationships with confidence.

The concept of attachment arises from the work of John Bowlby. He firmly believed that this attachment had to occur in the first two and a half years of life. Later research, however, has shown that this is not the case. Children who have, for example, been in institutional care for their early life can learn to form attachments within a loving and caring adoptive family. Bowlby emphasised the one strong attachment with the mother or primary care-giver; it is now recognised that children can make many attachments. One of them will be with you. You can provide them with the trust, the affection, the love and the warmth that they need to experience if they are to become secure and confident people.

Phases of attachment

The phases of attachment noted below are based on the work and findings of John Bowlby.

1. *Early months of life*: the baby is happy to have his needs met by anyone.

2. *5/7 months onwards*: the baby prefers to have his needs met by his mother or other important care-giver. This is the beginning of attachment.

3. *7/9 months onwards*: the baby crawls towards the mother or important care-giver, and frequently returns to her for contact. He may cry if this person leaves the room. He may become wary of unfamiliar people.

4. *2/3 years onwards*: the partnership between the mother and the child starts to include times when the child can meet the mother's needs and can for example wait for her to return. This is referred to as a goal-corrected partnership.

5. *School-aged children onwards*: the relationship between the child and the mother is based on more abstract conditions such as affection and trust.

The sorts of behaviour that encourage the formation of a strong attachment between the mother and her child have been described as:

> '*The quality and sensitivity of mother-infant face-to-face interaction ... the mother treating her infant as an individual with a mind, rather than just as a creature with needs to be satisfied ... responding to an infant's inferred state of mind, rather than simply their behaviour.*'

(Smith et al., 2003, pp 97 and 98)

They could equally well describe how you should interact with the children in your care, so that they form a sound relationship with you, built on that same concept of trust and affection.

Making Relationships: Effective practice: 16–26 months

Give your full attention when young children look to you for a response.

- Always look at the child when he is talking to you.

- Greet children with a smile and good eye contact.

- Ask the child what *he* thinks of a piece of work he has done, rather than simply telling him your opinion.

- Ask children which colour apron, flavour of juice, etc. they would like. Don't assume that you know what they want.

- Allow children to change their mind.

- If you have to say 'No' or 'Stop it' always add an explanation as to what they shouldn't do and then what they should be doing instead, or an explanation of why you said 'No' or 'Stop'.

- Be consistent.

- Be a good listener.

- Put yourself in the child's shoes. What did it feel like when you started this new job and had to spend all day with people you'd never met before, where you didn't know the routines or where things were kept?

  'The child who gets the best from nursery is the child who has a solid base of trust in friendly adults.'

  (Miller, 1992, p 25)

Relationships with peers

You will notice a clear pattern of relationship development in your children as you observe them playing.

- The baby is centred on himself and his own needs. This is solitary play.

- The toddler will play near other children. He may be using the same resource, but he will be engaged in his own play. You may notice him watching what others are doing and then copying them. This is parallel play.

- The toddler then starts to play with other children at the same activity. He may want all of the pieces for himself, he may find it difficult to share, but he is signalling his readiness to work in partnership. This is sometimes described as associative play.

- As children reach the age for starting school they may begin to play in a more cooperative way, each helping the other, each carrying out part of the activity and completing it between them. This is cooperative play.

Responding to children who struggle with relationships

First of all you have to identify the possible cause of this struggle. You have to know your children and their family circumstances if you are to help them in a useful way.

> *Making Relationships: Look, listen and note: 30–50 months*
>
> Children who like to be with others, and those who need help to join in.

There may be some simple steps you can take to help. You may need to give a little more focus on some aspect of behaviour support for some children.

TOP TIP!

Sometimes you will be aware of serious family issues that you should hand over to more appropriate authorities such as Social Services or Children's Mental Health (CAMHS) teams. Involve your special educational needs coordinator (SENCO) if there are serious concerns; she will have the contacts and the experience to help you.

Competitive children

Children are competitive – it is part of the struggle for survival, this need for self-preservation. Too often adults intervene too quickly in children's squabbles. They don't allow children the chance to sort things out for themselves.

Behaviour and Self-control: Effective practice: 40–60+ months

Involve children in identifying issues and finding solutions.

Children need to work out how to relate to other children. They have to learn about give and take, and that they can't always be the winners. Watch, observe and be ready to intervene, particularly if someone is getting hurt, but let them have a chance to reach their own conclusion.

TOP TIP!

If you have to intervene remember these few guidelines:

Give a firm but quiet instruction reminding the children of the setting's routine: 'Freddie, no hitting.'

Don't provide an audience. If necessary remove other children who are watching, maybe supporting one child against another, or generally encouraging the argument to develop.

Don't get drawn into their battle. Speak firmly in a quiet voice. Use as few words as possible. The time for a lengthy discussion is later when everyone has calmed down. Separate them, and engage them in alternative activities, each in the care of an adult, until they have calmed down.

When everyone is calm, talk about the alternative strategies they could have chosen to use for sorting out the problem. Each child can be asked to think of an alternative action they could have taken. Discuss both options. Are these alternatives better than what actually happened? Why?

There are times when you want to encourage competition. One way to introduce this is to encourage the children to compete against themselves, by practising some activity or skill until they can do it better, or faster, or more neatly – whatever is appropriate.

Why not try this?

Friendly competition

Set a challenge where everyone might be the winner. Remind the children that you are looking to see who can complete the challenge, not just who is first to complete it.

Stretch two tapes on the grass to mark a starting and a finishing line.

- Who can run all the way to this line?
- Who can jump all the way?
- Who can roll all the way?
- Who can hop all the way?
- Who can do it quickly?
- Who can do a funny walk all the way?
- Who can walk like a duck all the way?
- Who can run all the way with a bean bag on their head?
- Who can walk backwards to the line?

Only children

Only children may need to learn how to relate to other children who won't necessarily make allowances as adults do. Other children may squabble or fight over possession of some toy, which can distress a child who has been used to adults who usually don't do this. This may be a new experience for these children and you have to allow time for them to develop the social skills to cope. You will need to work with them on how to share, how to take turns and how to wait for attention.

Children who won't share their friend

Some children have a friend, but they want exclusive access to this friend. The friend isn't allowed to go off and play with any one else, and no one else is allowed to join in their games. When one child is calling the tune like this it can feel very threatening to the other child, even if he basically likes his friend and wants to spend some of the time with him.

At issue here is the child's need to have control, and it is this that you need to deal with. He has to learn that he can't control others.

Why not try this?

Two into three will go

Start by setting up an activity for three children, the two friends plus one other. Let's call them Alex – who dominates, Ben – who is dominated, and Carl – who is a cheerful boy with lots of friends. You need to choose a calm, outgoing child for this to work. An activity such as sand or water is a good one. Let the three play there for a time and then call Alex away. Involve him in an activity where he is alone with you, having lots of attention. He may be anxiously watching the other two to see how they get on. Don't keep him with you for very long, and then let him go back to the others. Now take Carl to work with you so that Ben and Alex have some time together.

Repeat this scenario on many occasions and in different activities, maybe with a different third child. Gradually increase the length of time that Alex is removed and Ben can play and work with other children.

Children who can't find a friend

Some children find it difficult to find a friend at all. They may shrink away from physical contact with others.

TOP TIP!

If any child persistently avoids any contact with adults or children, it may be a case where you should seek help. Has the child been a victim of abuse? Check with your manager and get her opinion first, and if necessary act in accordance with your setting's safeguarding children procedures.

Some children may make inappropriate advances towards the others. Like Beth in the following box.

Reflecting on practice

Beth, aged 4.5 years

Beth started school from a home where she was the only child of a second marriage, and where there were other grown-up children, resulting in lots of adult attention. She hadn't attended any pre-school settings. She would pin children up against the wall or in corners, smiling, trying to be

→

their friend. They were frightened by this; they already had some established friendships from their pre-school days, and so were unwilling to accept Beth as their friend.

The teacher began by involving Beth with one other child at a time in table-based activities. The table formed a physical barrier which maintained the level of accepted 'space' between people that is preferred in this culture. This helped the other child to feel safe.

Beth would be asked to help another child in activities such as carrying out the big basket of balls for PE – again this was a cooperative act that had a clearly defined personal space built into it.

Because Beth was particularly good at fastening shoes she would be asked to help others who were still struggling with this task, giving her a positive image in the eyes of the other children.

At the same time, PSE included work on friendships – what they mean, how we relate to other people, behaviours that are and are not suitable: 'Let's role play what you do when you meet your friend. Now let's do meeting the dentist when she comes into school. Or the man who serves you in the shop.' They talked about what the differences are and how some approaches are much better than others. Beth needed to learn how to greet other children if she was to be successful in making a friend.

Consider the following:

1. If there was no intervention to help Beth what do you think would happen?
2. What would her place be in the social group of the class?
3. How would she cope out on the playground?

Some children will respond more easily if they have a younger child to play with. They may be able to help a younger child with his activity: 'George finds it hard to cut these ribbon strips up for his collage. Could you help him?' They may enjoy showing a child how to play a board game, or helping him with a jigsaw.

Children who are aggressive towards others

It is important that you separate out what is real aggression and what is in fact rough-and-tumble play. You may not want either of these in the setting, but your attitude to these events needs to be distinctly different.

● Rough-and-tumble is part of children's play, possibly more so with boys than girls. You only have to watch young animals interacting with their litter mates to see this as a natural event.

● Aggression towards other children is more likely to involve hitting or kicking, name calling and hair pulling. All are activities designed to hurt the other person.

> **TOP TIP!**
>
> *To help you identify whether you are watching rough-and-tumble play or aggression, look at the expression on the child's face. The rough-and-tumble will be carried out with a smile or laughter, whereas the real aggression will be accompanied by frowns and grimaces, narrowed eyes and pursed lips.*

You have a choice of responses to aggression You can act in a way that simply ends the conflict – 'Stop that, you are hurting Amy', 'Don't do that or you'll break the garage' – or you can deal with the children by helping them to think of other ways to sort things out, or suggest ways that they can work together in a more cooperative and friendly fashion.

Research suggests a number of reasons for aggression in children. These include genetic factors (having a temperament that leads to aggressive behaviour), low self-esteem (this may cause the child to feel insecure and therefore ready to hit out at others), or home circumstances (when the child misses out on effective discipline or warmth and affection, or regularly sees aggression used as a way to resolve disagreements).

Apart from issues of low self-esteem, these are factors in which you will have little chance to intervene. If the parents ask you for advice, you can make sure that you know how and where to get the contact details for them. Or you can find out about help for parents through your contacts with your school medical team, or the health visitor, by discussing the problem with them and asking them if they can follow it up with the family. In preparation for such enquiries you can ask your medical contact if they have a card or leaflet that they can pin up on a notice board that parents can see.

Activities to help children develop partnerships with other children

Rowing boats

Children sit on the floor, legs straight out in front of them, facing their partner. They stretch forward and hold hands, rocking gently forwards and backwards as you all sing: *Row, row, row your boat,* or *See-saw, Margery daw.*

Hands together

Stand facing each other, sing and do the actions.

Hands together, clap *(Slap own thighs – on 'hands', clap own hands – on 'together', clap hands with the partner, both hands at once – on 'clap').*

Hands together, clap *(as above).*

Hands together clap, clap, *(as above, but for the 'clap, clap', clap each other's left hand for one 'clap' and the right hand for the second 'clap'; this means crossing hands as you clap).*

Hands together, clap *(as first line).*

Throw and catch

Any throwing and catching game promotes cooperation. To get children to help each other, rather than compete, provide an incentive.

For example, 'Count your catches'. Every time you get to five without dropping the ball or bean bag, you put a counter or cube into the bucket. Which pair of children can get ten counters in their bucket? Make sure you take it in turns – swap places after each counter goes in the bucket.

Rhymes for two

Learn some rhymes where there are two speakers, and take one part each:

Two little dicky birds

Miss Polly had a dolly

Work as a whole group to learn them, then divide into pairs to practise saying them – speaking together for the narrative and individually for the two characters.

Musical duo

Let the children work in pairs, each with a musical instrument, to play a simple tune.

Hickory Dickory Dock: one child plays the rhythm on the tambourine as they sing the words. The other child adds the 'tick, tock' with the drum – gently – at the end of each line, and a loud bang on the drum for the 'one' being struck.

Ding, dong, bell: each child has a different chime bar. They play alternately to represent the chiming of the bell, as they say the rhyme.

When is it bullying?

Bullying is behaviour towards another person that is designed to frighten or intimidate them and which is intentional and sustained.

Dealing with bullying

Sometimes relationships can turn very nasty. If you are to comply with the requirements of the *Every Child Matters* (www.dcsf.gov.uk) agenda then you have to be concerned about bullying and make every effort to prevent it or deal with it. It is connected with 'staying safe' as well as with 'making a positive contribution'. Children are expected to learn how to 'form positive relationships and not to bully or discriminate'.

There are a number of related issues that need to be considered when you are thinking about bullying.

● You have to know how you will deal with bullying when it occurs, with some form of punishment or consequence that shows the bullying child that this sort of behaviour is not acceptable at any level or at any time.

Most schools and settings will have an agreed system for dealing with cases of bullying, with specific records to keep. Make yourself familiar with these processes and make sure that you apply them rigorously. They will include sanctions, possibly having a meeting with the parents and child together, setting targets for behaviour and monitoring the child, especially when he is out of the classroom.

● You have to think about how you will deal with the victim at the time.

The victim will be in need of reassurance – that he has done the right thing in telling you about the bullying, and that he will be protected from further incidents.

● It is also important to think about ways that you can work towards preventing it in the first place, or avoiding any repeat of the bullying behaviour, so that some children don't become bullies and that others don't become victims.

This behaviour won't go away unless you are prepared to face it. You will have to support bullies and victims alike in order that they can modify the way they relate to other children. The longer-term scenario is that you will have to work with both of these children to change their future behaviour.

L. Alan Sroufe

L. Alan Sroufe is the William Harris Professor of Childhood Studies at Minnesota University. During his research into attachment he and his students

→

took a group of four year olds and paired them off with same-sex play-mates. He included all combinations of attachment types and then observed their behaviour. (This study is summed up in Karen,1998.) See page 70 in this chapter for a description of the attachment types.

Sroufe noticed that:

● Children who are securely attached tend to be more sensitive to the needs of their friends and peers. Whatever the type of child they mix with, they are able to cope with the other child's anxieties, and still make positive relationships. They can make allowances for other children's preferences, and initiate activities. They support other more vulnerable children and generally make good friendships. At the same time they don't allow themselves to be bullied.

● Children with insecure attachments are those most likely to become either the bully or the victim. They are less sociable than securely attached children and less popular. Avoidant children can sometimes take advantage of their less competent peers, and don't seem interested in being close to others. Ambivalent children are often not very good at forming relationships even though they would like to be able to do this. They get on better with secure children who help the relationship to develop, but struggle to form positive relationships with anxiously attached children.

Why do children bully?

It's to do with power and relationships and self-image.

'The child's understanding of relationships can only be from the relationships he's experienced.'

(Sroufe, 1989, cited in Karen, 1998)

Some children have seen adults use their greater size and power to dominate. They come to believe that they can, maybe even should, also use their size and power in this way. If there are children who are physically smaller or younger than them, or if they find children who are vulnerable, they may build their relationship with them on power and domination. Some children have been constantly belittled by the adults around them to the point where they choose to hurt others first as a form of self-protection.

Some children haven't developed the social skills that allow them to make friends and relate to other people in acceptable ways. Some children show little empathy for other people, and don't consider the consequences of their actions on their victims.

The bullying behaviour can be a sign that the child's emotional needs are not being met. These children are likely to grow into adults who rely on aggression as a way of expressing their own needs or views unless someone is prepared to step in and help them change.

Making Relationships: Look, listen and note: 40–60+ months

Children's relationships with other children and adults.

Empowering children to protect themselves

If there are no victims available, there can be no bullying. If children are to avoid becoming the victim of a bully you need to give them the skills to protect themselves. Children who are not securely attached or children with low self-esteem are more likely to become victims. You will be working with them already to address these issues but every child also needs to have some basic tools that they can use if another child ever attempts to bully them.

- They need to know how to recognise bullying behaviour.
- They need to know how to respond.
- They need the language to describe their feelings.
- They need to know that they will be taken seriously.

Behaviour and Self-control: Effective practice: 22–36 months

Help children to understand their rights to be kept safe by others, and encourage them to talk about ways to avoid hurting or harming others.

Why not try this?

Circle Time

This is a good time to practise talking about emotions and feelings.

Each child in turn completes the sentence:

→

'I feel happy when ...'

'I feel scared when ...'

Tell the others to listen carefully, and, 'If you agree, touch your knee'.

Recognising bullying behaviour

Stories shared in PSE time can be a way of introducing young children to the fact that there are some people who will act in unkind ways towards others. When adults know about this they will deal with it or help you to deal with it. If the adult doesn't know then they can't help you.

There are examples of suitable books for this in the *Going further* section at the end of this chapter.

Behaviour and Self-control: Planning and resourcing: 40–60+ months

Provide books with stories about characters that follow or break rules, and the effects of their behaviour on others.

Talk about good and bad secrets. Explain that if a child is behaving in mean or nasty ways we should all be helping them to learn how to behave in kind and friendly ways. Adults can only help if they know about the unkind behaviour. So it is important to share this knowledge with your teacher or one of the adults. It should never be a secret.

Taking it seriously

If a child tells you he has been bullied or is scared or upset by the presence of a particular child, find a quiet space where you can ask about what has happened, when and who did it.

Ask the child how he is feeling.

Tell him that you are going to help him to keep safe.

Discuss the issue with his parents so that you can tell them what has happened and what you are doing about it.

Provide a buddy for the child who has been a victim for a few days until his confidence returns.

Make other staff aware so that they can also keep an eye on the situation.

Talk to the child who had been accused of bullying. Find out the other side of the story.

Talk to the parents of the child who has been accused of bullying about what has happened and how you and they can work together to help to resolve the situation at this early stage, before it becomes entrenched behaviour.

Working with the child who bullies

If the reason for this sort of behaviour is linked to an attachment problem you will need to ask for help from the SENCO. She in turn may need help from children's mental health services. It could be a long-term or family issue that is beyond your remit.

If the child has low self-esteem you can go a long way towards helping to relieve this. There are ideas in Chapter 6 for this, but basically your aim is to make the child feel that he has some worth, that he is valued and that he matters to you and the group.

If the child has poor social skills there are many practical things you can do to help him. There are ideas in Chapters 2, 7 and 9. Your aim is to teach him more appropriate ways to relate to other children, through being able to share, to take turns and to be a friend.

Your aim is to deal with the child who bullies in a constructive way to help him change, whilst responding with firmness to his unacceptable behaviour. You have to show the child that you have a strict boundary in this setting, that bullying is never acceptable or excusable. A firm approach helps the child who is insecurely attached. It shows him that you are reliable and trustworthy. If he is to start to develop an attachment with you, then trust is one thing that there has to be between you.

Developing a professional Code of Conduct within the setting

At some point you are going to have to manage other adults. You may be responsible for a student, a volunteer parent helper, a new member of staff – and eventually you will be a line manager with all the responsibilities that are involved in that role. You will have to think about how you will behave if you are to be effective in this new role.

Why not try this?

Task 1

Think about a manager that you have enjoyed working for.

How did they speak to you?

What did they do when you asked yet another question?

What was their reaction when you got something wrong?

Did you feel able to tell them when you found something hard, or didn't feel that you were coping well with a particular child or parent?

Task 2

Think about a manager that you didn't enjoy working for.

Compare their behaviour with that of the manager you admired.

Did you feel that you performed well for this person?

Did your fear or dislike of them affect you – at work or privately?

Task 3

Think about your own style of management.

What impression do you want to leave with the person you are managing?

How will they think of you?

Which category will they put you in?

Tips for managing adults

- Make sure that the person has a mixture of interesting and routine tasks. You don't want them to feel used by giving them only mundane, repetitive tasks. Neither do you want them to think they are above doing some of those tasks. Variety will maintain their interest.

- You have to motivate the person to want to do well. Speak in positive ways about the tasks they have to do. Explain how they fit into the curriculum or the routines of the setting and the importance they have for the children. You want the person to be enthusiastic about their role. You also want to know that they are committed to the task you have set them.

- When people have responsibility they often 'grow into' the job. When you can sense that the person is ready to take on more, tell them that this is what you believe about them, give them the responsibility and, in the first instance, keep an eye on them. Step in if things go wrong, but only after you have given them a chance to show what they can achieve by themselves, or correct their own mistakes.

- Show that you appreciate what they have done and how they have done it. Notice what they do and comment on it so that they are aware that you are observing their practice, but that they are doing the right things.

- Give feedback so that the person knows:

  - how well they are doing;

  - any areas where they need to change or modify their approach;

  - things that you want them to try next in order to increase their skills.

In touch with parents – building the relationship

The relationship you have with parents will take many forms; it will vary from one family to another; it will change with different stages of the child's education and because of changing home circumstances. Your over-arching aim is to have a relationship built on trust and respect, both ways.

Behaviour and Self-control: Planning and resourcing: 16–26 months

Share policies and practice with parents, ensuring an accurate two-way exchange of information, through an interpreter or through translated materials where necessary.

Strengthening the relationship between your setting and the families

When the relationship between school and home is on a firm, tolerant and friendly footing it makes it much easier for the child to move between the two places, the two sets of routines and the two sets of adults. In its turn this encourages the child to behave well, to know that he is pleasing both sets of adults in his life. And when things go wrong it's good to know that you can expect support from the parent.

Behaviour and Self-control: Effective practice: birth–11 months

Find out as much as you can from parents about young babies before they join the setting, so that the routines you follow are familiar and comforting.

Be available, be welcoming

- Induction meetings before the child even starts with you give parents a considerable amount of one-to-one time with you. Once the child is settled this may be reduced to ten minutes at the termly parents' meeting. So, making the most of informal times to talk with parents is vital. Organise your time so that you can be available at the start or end of the day to talk with parents about their child.

- If a parent is anxious about their child – perhaps he said he didn't feel well as they came into school, or the cat died last night – make an arrangement whereby the parent can phone or text you during the day to check how things are going.

TOP TIP!

Meeting parents at the end of the day is preferable and often easier to organise, and it allows for more time. Explain this to parents – you can see me now for a few minutes, but if you would like to spend a little longer then it would be great if you can come in after the session.

Encourage partnership

- Parents know their children well. They can provide you with an insight into how their child 'works', what he likes doing, what upsets him, how he views the world. Parents like to talk about their children. They appreciate it when they know that you also find their child interesting and worth caring about. Maintain this openness as a way of understanding the child, because only then can you help him when he struggles with his work, emotions or behaviour. Let the parents know about their child's behaviour as well as their work. Let them know if something has upset their child, or if they behaved more 'like his old self' after a period of illness or unsettled behaviour following a family crisis.

- Explain what you are doing – no doubt your weekly plans are displayed where parents can see them. Your newsletters will tell parents about new developments, changes or new staff. But don't forget that as well as asking for help with the next cooking session, you can use letters home to ask for help and support in maintaining good behaviour.

Dear parents,

I'm sorry to have to tell you that in the past week we have had to speak to lots of the children about kicking. We think they are copying the behaviour of one of the cartoon characters that they like to watch. We have talked to them about the difference between what characters in stories, or on television, can do and the reality of other children getting hurt. Could you please find time to repeat this message with your child over the weekend. We would be very grateful for your support on this.

Many thanks,

Mary Smith

A follow-up letter the next week to give the results, and hopefully to thank the parents for their support in solving this problem, will always be appreciated.

Be supportive

One of the things that you can try to do is to anticipate, and then try to meet, parents' needs.

● If you have a number of children with the same behavioural issues, or parents tell you about similar problems that they are having with their children's behaviour – perhaps poor sleep patterns or jealousy towards a new baby – arrange for some help. Ask your local health visitor, school nurse or the CAMHS team if they can come to the setting and run a workshop for your parents.

Reflecting on practice

When you need to get in touch

If there are problems with a child's behaviour, or you have concerns over sudden changes in the child's behaviour, you will need to talk to the parents. This is best done in private, and at an agreed time, so that you can be prepared and can set a relaxed atmosphere of cooperation, not antagonism. Consider how you will arrange this with the parent. You want to be discreet so you may decide to write to the parents, rather than approaching them in front of all the other parents to make the appointment.

You could phone or text the parent. However, this can result in them asking you what it's about, and before you realise it, you are holding the discussion over the phone. It isn't the best way of dealing with potentially sensitive issues.

Where schools know that they have children whose home language is not English they often have some mechanism for translating important letters, or having a bilingual friend or family member present during parent–teacher interviews. Find out about these from your manager or the secretary as it may take time to arrange.

→

What about those parents who can't read? You may not know who these are. Most of them will have their own strategies for getting by. Some parents may eventually divulge this information if you build a strong relationship with them. In the mean time, make your letters straightforward. Put important dates or times, or the phone number you want them to ring to make the appointment, in bold print so that this can be picked out from the rest of the document more easily.

Consider the following:

1. Do you know if any of your parents need help to read or understand the information you send them?

2. How do you deal with sensitive matters in ways that save everyone from embarrassment?

Conclusion

The ability to make relationships with others is a key part of living in a society and playing a role within that society. It is a skill that some children may need help with if they are to form the kinds of relationships that are mutually satisfying, and based on tolerance and respect. Your role is first of all to set an example in the way that you relate to the children, to your colleagues and to the parents. At the same time you will be alert to the children's early attempts at making friends and help them if that proves necessary.

Key ideas summary

You now know that if you want to encourage strong and positive relationships within your setting you have to:

- Recognise the different ways in which children may be attached to their main care-giver.

- Deal with signs of aggression or dominance that is affecting other children.

- Help children to work in cooperative ways.

- Be pro-active in helping children to make friends.

- Find out why any child is bullying others and respond to those needs.

- Deal with the victims of bullying.

- Be consistent and reliable.

Going further

Search the website of the Letterbox Library for books about bullying. Their books are listed by theme, and a suitable age range for each book is given. You can order them online at www.letterboxlibrary.com

For talking about bullying with 3 to 6 year olds you could try:

Ross, T. (2006) *Is it Because?* London: Andersen Press.

Foreman, J. and Foreman, M. (2008) *Say Hello,* London: Walker Books.

Moore, M. (2008) *Ben the Bully,* London: Hachette.

Simon, F. (2005) *Hugo and the Bully Frogs,* London: Gullane.

Social and Emotional Aspects of Learning (SEAL) is a government initiative that started in the secondary sector but is now available for all age groups. A useful resource that you can download is *Say no to bullying,* which is one of the titles offered as part of the EYFS curriculum materials for SEAL. The same titles appear for each year group, so look for the Red Set, which has been planned for Early Years settings:

www.nationalstrategies.standards.dcsf.gov.uk/inclusion/behaviourandattend
    anceandseal/curriculummaterials

Choose the option for Early Years or the EYFS stage to download the Red set of activities.

Squirrel says

It was still quite early. Squirrel had just woken up when he heard the sound of a reversing lorry. 'Beep! Beep! This vehicle is reversing' went the mechanical voice. Squirrel got up and went to look out of his living-room window. A huge van, with 'Rats Removals' in red letters on its side, was reversing towards the main door. Last week the Vole family had moved to a new house nearer to the river. This must be the new people who were coming to live in their old flat.

By the time Squirrel had dressed and sat down for his breakfast the removal rats were starting to unload the furniture. The day was warming up and the rats were getting very red in the face as they carted the heavy boxes up the stairs to number 8. Squirrel got some mugs out of his cupboard and filled →

them with orange juice, put them on his round tray and carried them carefully down to the van. 'Thought you would like a drink,' he called out to the rats. 'Thanks, mate,' said the rats, eagerly drinking the juice.

At that moment an old car drove up, parked in one of the bays and out tumbled two small hedgehogs, one slightly larger hedgehog, a mother hedgehog carrying a little tiny baby hedgehog, and last of all, father hedgehog, locking the car after him. Over on the grass some of the other children from the flats were sorting themselves into two teams ready to play football. Squirrel called over to them.

'Fran, Fergus, and you others, come and meet your new neighbours.'

The children came over and said 'Hi,' to the hedgehog children.

'Do you want to come and play?' asked Fran.

'Can we, Mum?' asked the biggest hedgehog.

'Of course, you can, as long as you stay on the grass and don't go wandering off.'

'We won't', chorused the hedgehog children, and went off to play with their new friends. Squirrel asked Mr and Mrs Hedgehog if they would like to sit in his flat with a cup of tea while the rats finished carrying all their boxes and furniture up to the flat.

'That would be wonderful,' they said.

Squirrel says,

'Be ready to make new friends feel welcome.'

5

Develop self-control and emotional balance

What this chapter will explore:

- How to recognise a child's emotional maturity
- How to measure a child's emotional maturity
- The role of the adult in supporting the child's emotional development
- How to deal with emotional outbursts in the setting
- Ideas for activities to support emotional development

This chapter will concentrate on ways to recognise and support your children's emotional development, another factor influencing the child's ability to behave in appropriate ways.

The ultimate aim of emotional development is for a person to become emotionally competent, or emotionally balanced. There are two sides to this:

1. Each person needs to be able to deal with his own emotions, recognising that he has different feelings, that it is OK to have these feelings or emotions, and that they can be controlled.

2. Each person should be able to recognise the fact that other people also have emotions, that they are entitled to have them, and that they need to have the skills to deal with them and their expression.

The children in your early years settings will be somewhere along the path to achieving this level, although they are unlikely to actually attain emotional competence at this early stage of their lives.

Recognising emotional development

Your aim is that your children will be emotionally competent, so that they can deal with the good and the bad experiences they will have in their lifetime. But do you know the stages that children go through as they move towards this emotional competency?

It is relatively straightforward to check the progress of a child's development in things such as vocabulary and language use, physical growth or his acquisition of new facts and skills, but how do you check his emotional development? It is possible to develop a set of guidelines against which you can check his emotional progress (although it will never be as clear as measuring height or weight). You should be able to do this by the end of this chapter.

This information will be useful to you, helping you to understand some aspects of the child's behaviour.

> **TOP TIP!**
>
> *When you know about the child's emotional status and his emotional capacities (what he is and isn't yet capable of dealing with) you will be able to respond in helpful and supportive ways.*

The first step is to consider how you observe the emotions displayed by your children.

Observing emotional development

Whenever you observe children you will be *looking* at them, but it is also necessary that you take notice of what you are looking at and that you *interpret* these things against your chosen criteria. So remember to:

- look;
- notice;
- interpret.

When you are concentrating on observing a child's behaviour you should be aware of the children's:

- facial expressions;
- bodily presentations;
- physiological changes.

You may also be aware of children talking about their feelings, and these verbal exchanges or comments will be dealt with later in this chapter.

And what will you see? The following box includes some of the possibilities, and by concentrating on these you should be able to really notice what your children are showing you about their emotional state and, through your interpretation of this, begin to identify the stages of their emotional development.

Some signs that the child is feeling an emotion

Facial expressions:

- Eyes – wide open, narrowed, staring, closed, tearful.
- Eyebrows – raised, lowered, frowning.
- Nose – wrinkled, nostrils flared or narrowed.
- Mouth – wide open, tight shut, corners raised, corners lowered, lips taut in a square shape.

Other physical manifestations:

- Arms – outstretched, tight across chest.
- Head – up high, lowered, cast down, face covered by hands.
- Stance – upright and tall, shrunken and bent over, cowering.
- Shoulders – firmly back, bowed, dropped.

→

Physiological changes:

- Skin – flushed, pale.
- Breathing – regular, irregular, deep, gasping.
- Heart rate/pulse – raised, lowered.

In order to then interpret these observations you need to know about early emotional development. Here is a summary of some aspects that will be of use.

Early emotions

The first emotions (psychologists describe these as *primary emotions*) provide the new-born baby with some important survival strategies. Some of these emotions help the baby to avoid dangerous or harmful situations. Others encourage the adults around the baby to offer care, love, comfort and support.

> 'Early emotion is very much about pushing people away or drawing them closer.'

> (Gerhardt, 2004, p 19)

Schaffer (2004, p 127) lists the earliest emotions as fear, anger, surprise, disgust, joy and sadness. Smith et al. (2003) add happiness, interest and pain to this list. Fancourt (2000) suggests that the more complex emotions of joy, sadness, assertiveness and anger don't appear until the baby is about two months old.

Self-confidence and Self-esteem: Look, listen and note: 8–20 months

The sounds, words and actions that babies use to show feelings such as pleasure, excitement, frustration or anger.

If you think of these early emotions in terms of their survival potential you will realise how important they are to these vulnerable babies to keep them safe. For example:

- *Fear* shows that they can respond to potential danger or to anyone who wishes to hurt them. At this early stage in life babies express fear by crying or widening their eyes, causing the mother or care-giver to respond to the child and offer comfort or deal with the danger.

- A cry of *pain* likewise stirs the care-giver into action.

- It is important that babies avoid eating anything harmful, and so they are able to express *disgust* at unusual foods or unpleasant things they put in their mouths.

Babies smile at the care-giver, which in turn evokes a warm feeling in that other person, who then wants to love and please the baby, so perpetuating a cycle of trust and security. This cycle of interaction is the beginning of the relationship that will develop appropriate emotional competence.

Fancourt (2000) describes the emotions that a baby shows in the first week of life as 'contentment' or 'distress'. This is also discussed in Gerhardt (2004), who talks about the new-born baby as having 'global feelings' that she describes as 'distress' and 'discomfort' at one end of the emotional spectrum and 'content-ment' and 'comfort' at the other. The main aim of anybody with caring responsibilities is to hard-wire into the child's brain a sense of comfort and con-tentment. Contentment occurs when adults respond to the baby's needs, and distress is shown when there is no apparent response.

TOP TIP!

Keep in your mind the fact that a baby doesn't have a time frame or any concept of time. He doesn't comprehend the idea that someone will be there 'in a minute'; he can't understand that you have heard him cry and gone off to prepare his feed, and so he can easily become distressed by what he senses as a lack of response.

Self-confidence and Self-esteem: Effective practice: birth–11 months

Talk to a young baby when you cannot give them your direct attention, so that they are aware of your interest and your presence nearby.

Later emotions

By the age of two or three years the child is very much aware of himself as an individual. You will know this stage has been reached when the child recognises himself in a mirror. As a very young baby he considered himself and his mother to be one person and viewed his toes as a separate plaything! But this is replaced at this time with a sense of individuality, as shown by his determination to have his own way and the temper tantrums that become a big feature of his emotional life. Once he knows he is a separate person he is able to evaluate himself, he knows when he has achieved something to be proud of, and he also knows when he has done something wrong. This self-knowledge means that he can now experience a new range of emotions. He can now display the emotions that Schaffer (2004) identifies as pride, guilt, shame and embarrassment.

Emotions that you might expect to see in young children

fear	sadness	anger
anger	happiness	pride
surprise	interest	guilt
disgust	pain	shame
joy	assertiveness	embarrassment

Another development at this stage is that children are now able to blend emotions so that they can sometimes show more than one at a time. They can also disguise their emotions or show them in more subtle ways as they learn to react in ways that their society finds appropriate. It is now much more difficult as an observer to identify the emotional state that the children are in. They may be saying thank you and looking pleased at the gift, when underneath they are disappointed that it isn't what they were hoping for. The child who is constantly rejected or ignored at home may have learnt to shut off his feeling of isolation, and gives the appearance that he is happy to be playing by himself.

Fortunately the child is now developing a new skill. He can talk with increasing complexity of thought and language, so he can give voice to his emotions and discuss feelings with the adults or in the group if he so chooses. Some children may need sensitive encouragement to do this.

Why not try this?

Staff activity

1. Take two lists:

   - List 1: A copy of the ideas in the three sections of the box on pages 95–96: Some signs that the child is feeling an emotion.

   - List 2: The early emotions that children might show, followed by the later emotions, as given in the table above: Emotions that you might expect to see in young children.

2. Work as a group to match the emotions (List 2) to the signs (List 1). There may be more than one option for each sign.

Your aim is to produce a list that shows each emotion followed by its potential signs (see www.pearsoned.co.uk/essentialguides for further material on this activity).

Emotions and culture

Experiments carried out across different continents and with people from a variety of cultures show that the same early emotions are fairly standard to all people, and they are expressed in similar ways. Psychologists and anthropologists alike have debated the question of whether our emotions are to do with nature (part of our evolution and thus common to all people) or nurture (specific to the culture that the child is born and raised within). Other aspects of body language, such as gestures, differ widely from one culture to another, but facial expressions are often similar. It is worth noting that these same facial expressions are also seen in children who are born deaf and blind. There is an argument that this is because of the limits or possibilities of our physiology – there are only so many ways you can move particular muscles in your cheeks, for example – but perhaps they are part of our common genetic make-up.

When people from different cultures 'read' emotions in the facial expressions of others they give similar interpretations. It seems as if the manner of expressing these early emotions is common to all people.

Reflecting on practice

Frankie, aged 3.2 years

This is an example of 'noticing' rather than 'looking' when you are observing a child.

Frankie came happily to nursery. He sat at the edge of the room and simply watched the children playing. He smiled and seemed content, but didn't attempt to join in. His key worker's interpretation of this emotional presentation was that things weren't right, even if Frankie was apparently happy and well behaved.

She made a home visit and discovered that Frankie and his young mum lived high up in a tower block. His mum didn't take Frankie out to play or play with him at home. Instead he spent the day in front of the television – watching other people do things.

Talking with Frankie his key worker found that he didn't know that he could join in. He thought this was just another 'television', something that he watched and that he enjoyed watching. Once it was explained to him that he could join in, he was keen to mix with the other children in all the activities. His key worker made sure that she was there to support him as he made his early attempts at socialising. →

Consider the following:

When you have children who are always quiet and well behaved make sure that you pay attention to them – are they mixing well, are they taking advantage of the learning and play activities that you provide? Or are they existing on the sidelines of life in the setting?

Making Relationships: Planning and resourcing: 16–26 months

Regularly evaluate the way you respond to different children.

Talking about emotions

As children's language develops they start to use words to describe their own feelings – 'Me fright' or 'Hand hurt'. This will be noticed from about 18 months onwards, and by the age of 24 months is a common feature. At first the child mentions only his own emotional state; talking about the emotions they notice in others is not usually seen until the child is 30–36 months old. At this stage you may hear him tell you 'Mummy sad' or 'Sophie cry'. By this time his range of vocabulary is increasing, and this means that he can talk about internal feelings such as fear and anxiety as well as the more obvious visual expressions of emotion, such as laughter or crying.

Early emotional language development

- 18–24 months: begins to use words to describe own feelings
- 30–36 months: begins to talk about the feelings of other people

    begins to try to explain own feelings and those of other people
- 36 months+: begins to talk about internal feelings of self and others

The role of the adult

It is important to the child's emotional development that the adults around him make a conscious effort to provide him with the vocabulary that he needs if he is to talk about feelings and emotions. In the early stages of emotional language development the adult will need to verbalise the child's own feelings, providing him with the language and the vocabulary that he needs.

> **Making Relationships: Effective practice: 16–26 months**
>
> Help young children to label emotions such as sadness, or happiness, by talking to them about their own feelings and those of others.

Gerhardt (2004) describes this as the adult 'showing me my feelings': 'You look very sad today.' When you do this make sure that you use expressions such as 'look' rather than 'are'. You are telling him what you see rather than what he is (or maybe isn't) feeling.

> **Listening for signs of a child's emotional language development**
>
> ● Comments on own feelings.
> ● Comments on the feelings of others.
> ● Asks questions about emotions.
> ● Discusses possible causes of specific feelings.
> ● Shows empathy for another child or adult by words of support and understanding.

The adult continues to play a vital role, helping the child to broaden his vocabulary so that he can describe his emotions with increasing accuracy. By widening the children's vocabulary you are helping them to describe their own emotions more exactly and increasing their knowledge of the range of emotions that people might be experiencing or expressing.

> **TOP TIP!**
>
> *When his hand hurts, ask him if it is just sore, or painful, or tender – think of all the words we use to describe how we are feeling, and try to encourage the children to be more precise.*

If the child can't talk about his emotions he has to resort to behaviour to show what he is feeling – this is fine when he is happy but can cause huge problems for others if he is angry, or distress for himself if he is frightened. Language is one mechanism for helping him to understand his own emotions, and the emotions that others might be feeling. If you want children to be able to talk through their emotions rather than acting out their feelings, then you have to make sure they have the vocabulary to do this, as well as the opportunity, time and an adult available and ready to listen and discuss.

Talking about emotions may achieve the following:

- Enable a child to name and so identify his feelings.
- Help a child to understand his feelings, their causes and their effects.
- Comfort a child who is anxious by sharing his feelings with a supportive adult.
- Offer a child an explanation of what he is feeling, and why.
- Bring things out into the open where they can be dealt with.
- Reassure him about the way others are feeling.
- Help a child to find out what others might be feeling.
- Help the child to see that the same emotions are felt by other people as well as him.

Gender differences

It's often said that females are better at talking about their feelings than males. This is a commonly held belief, and some research is available to support this theory.

A study by Happe (1995) showed that even as young as three years old girls were better than boys at inferring what others might be thinking. Girls' greater ability to read body language, facial expressions and understand another person's feelings is described by Hall (1978). This may stem from the fact that girls show a greater interest in faces. In fact, it has been recorded that girl babies – from the moment of birth – look at faces for longer, particularly the eyes. In contrast boys prefer to look at inanimate objects (Connellan et al., 2001).

If you watch your children as they play you will notice differences between the way that girls and boys interact. Girls' play tends to take up less space than boys' play. This means that girls can indulge in conversations that are shared with only one or two others, that they can give eye contact and that their talk can be more intimate. This all lends itself to the sharing of emotions. Boys, on the other hand, play in larger groups using more space. This means that they tend to call to each other, often speaking only to give instructions or make expressive noises. This limits their chances of holding intimate discussions with their peers.

These innate tendencies have implications for early years practice; you may need to offer more encouragement to boys to join in with activities that include opportunities to talk about feelings.

> **Making Relationships: Planning and resourcing: 22–36 months**
>
> Create areas in which children can sit and chat with friends, such as a snug den.

The developing brain: dealing with emotions

The part of the brain that is first to receive an emotional stimulus is called the amygdala. This is more or less fully mature at birth. So the baby and young child can feel emotions and respond in automatic ways – the smile, the spitting out of unpleasant foods, screaming with fear, and so on.

The part of the brain that thinks about things is the frontal cortex. This isn't mature at birth. In fact it doesn't mature fully until we are adults. So the child is not able to rationalise his emotions. This is why you will see more outbursts of emotion in children and teenagers than in the average adult. Adults feel the emotions (through the amygdala) and then deal with them (through the frontal cortex). Children simply respond to the emotional stimulus.

The development of this ability to control emotions can be speeded up if adults help the children to show control. Every time you stimulate a set of brain cells they are strengthened. So the more an action is repeated the more it becomes a fixed pattern of behaviour in the child. This is called 'hard-wiring' the brain. If a child is punished harshly and repeatedly, he may become fearful of adults or aggressive towards them, for this is the pattern that is hard-wired. This is what the child expects and this is what the child learns to do. If you praise a child and encourage self-control then these are the feelings and patterns of behaviour that are hard-wired into the child. This hard-wiring is happening while the child is young, so it is the responsibility of those working with young children to aim to hard-wire into the child positive patterns of emotional control, which ultimately comes from feeling confident, secure, loved and cared for.

Reflecting on practice

Monitoring children's level of emotional development

There is no need for you to record this in the form of another set of boxes to tick. It is already part of your PSE assessment. What is important is that you monitor in order to be aware of the child's emotional level so that you can respond appropriately to the behaviour he exhibits.

When you have to deal with a child who is possibly angry, distressed, withdrawn or the victim of another child's anger, think before you respond. Take time to consider questions such as:

➡

- Is he only showing the primary (early) emotions? If so he is not going to understand me suggesting that he should feel ashamed of what he has just done.
- Does he have the maturity to self-evaluate his actions? At this stage he can feel extreme guilt if he breaks something, for example, and he may respond by hiding the evidence, especially if he has met with anger from adults when he's done this before.
- Can he talk about his own emotions yet?
- Can he discuss the possible reasons for his actions, or even the actions of other children?
- Is it worth having a discussion with him about his behaviour in a certain situation?

Consider the following:

Understanding the child means you can understand his behaviour and his actions and respond to them in appropriate ways.

Activities to help the children practise emotional balance

Used as part of your Personal, Social and Emotional development programme, these activities will help the children:

- recognise emotions – in themselves and in others;
- identify emotions – as their language skills develop this is an opportunity to refine their vocabulary so that they can name their feelings with increasing accuracy;
- deal with emotions – this is when you can offer non-emotional times to talk about feelings, and the ways that the feelings of other people can affect us.

Self-confidence and Self-esteem: Effective practice: 40–60+ months

Encourage children to share their feelings and talk about why they respond to experiences in particular ways.

Talking activities

Using puppets

There are many large figure puppets or persona dolls available that make ideal instruments for talking about feelings.

Start a Circle Time session by describing or enacting a sequence of events or a short storyline involving the puppet. Here are some ideas to start you off, but it would also be a good idea to replay any similar incident that you have had to deal with in the last day or two.

1. The puppet is coming to this setting for the first time.
2. The puppet has to come to school when his granny is visiting and he wanted to stay at home.
3. The puppet's hamster is ill/has died.
4. The puppet's birthday is tomorrow.
5. Someone has just broken the puppet's new toy that he brought to show everyone.
6. The puppet wants to play in the sand but there are already a lot of children in there, and there's no room for him. He has to wait.

Discuss the puppet's emotional state with the children. Here are some questions that you could use to start the discussion:

'What is he feeling?'

'The puppet is feeling ... today.'

'How do you know he is feeling like this?'

'Why does he feel like this?'

'Is there anything *he* could do about it?'

'Is there anything *we* could do to make the puppet feel better/happier? Or his mummy could do? Or his friend could do?'

'Is there anything we could say to the puppet?'

Allow time for the children to say something helpful or comforting to the puppet, letting them come out and speak directly to the puppet, which can be made to respond appropriately.

> ### Behaviour and Self-control: Planning and resourcing: 40–60+ months
>
> Encourage the children to think about issues from the viewpoint of others.

Ask the children to make a face like the puppet might make when he feels this way. Or you could ask them to stand or move like the puppet might do when he feels like this.

Hot-seating

This activity involves someone role playing a part and answering questions in that role. Start with an adult in the hot-seat until the children are familiar with the process. The children should be asking their own questions about the character's feelings, but again they will need to practise formulating questions. In this instance you want to concentrate on questions about feelings.

> ### Self-confidence and Self-esteem: Effective practice: 40–60+ months
>
> Support children's growing ability to express a wide range of feelings orally, and talk about their own experiences.

Have something to dress up in, or to hold, to show who is in the hot seat. You might adopt a special voice for your character.

Some ideas to begin with:

Cinderella (hold an invitation or a glittery sandal):

How did you feel when your sisters went off to the ball and left you at home?

Were you frightened when the Fairy Godmother appeared?

Do you like your sisters? Why? Why not?

Goldilocks (hold a bowl or wear an apron):

What did you feel like when you broke the chair?

Did you get scared when you heard the bears coming back?

An ugly sister (wear a ridiculous wig):

Why don't you like Cinderella?

Why did you try to get your large foot into the little glass slipper?

Were you sad when it didn't fit you? Why?

Creative activities

Paper plate faces

Each child should decorate two paper plates, one with a happy face and one with a sad face.

Teddy's tale Tell a story and ask the children to display the appropriate face as the story unfolds. Include plenty of things that go badly as well as things that turn out well, so that the children can change faces frequently.

Teddy was going out for walk.

He stepped into the street. The sun was shining.

He saw his friend Polar and waved to him. He was so busy looking at Polar that he didn't see the broken paving and tripped up, banging his nose.

He started to cry.

Polar came over to see how he was.

He helped Teddy to stand up and together they went to the ice cream van and bought two huge ice creams with chocolate and sprinkles.

And so on.

I feel like this ... The adult says something and the children show the appropriate plate face. Try:

When I have my friend round to tea I feel ...

When I have a pain I feel ...

When it is my birthday I feel ...

When I play on the swing with my friend I feel ...

When my baby brother giggles I feel ...

When my baby sister cries I feel ...

'Feelings' displays

What I feel like Take photographs of the children as they demonstrate different feelings. Mount them and add labels using the children's own words. 'I feel ... when ... '

Funny feelings Children could paint pictures of large faces. Cartoon drawings of faces can be good, simple examples of different emotional states. Cut some out and show them to the children before they start. Can they identify the emotions on the faces? Show them how to make up-turned mouths for smiles and down-turned mouths for sadness, open mouths for shock or horror; eyebrows can be straight, arched high for shock or making a v-shape for anger.

Songs and circle games

To the tune of 'Here we go round the mulberry bush'

1. Dance round in a ring with suitable expressions on the face, as you sing, 'The children are feeling … today'. Try: sad, happy, funny, cross, fed up.

2. 'This is the way I feel today, feel today, feel today

    I'm feeling very …'

Children demonstrate in face and posture the feeling that you say. Try: happy, angry, frightened.

To the tune of 'Peter hammers with one hammer' Use a name that is not one from your group of children.

> 'When Peter's feeling angry, angry, angry
>
> When Peter's feeling angry he looks like this.'

Make an appropriate 'face'.

Or Peter could be feeling happy, frightened or poorly.

To the tune of 'London Bridge is falling down' One child stands in the centre of a circle of children who sing as they dance round him:

> 'My friend Mark is feeling sad, etc.,
>
> How can I help him?'

The child in the centre points to someone in the circle who then comes into the middle. They join hands and dance together as those in the circle clap and sing:

> 'My friend Mark is feeling glad, etc.,
>
> Because Joanne helped him.'

The children swap places and the game continues.

Developing a professional Code of Conduct within the setting

Your code of conduct should contain some reference to the need for calm. If the adults can remain calm in the face of any disturbance, this is setting a superb example for the children. Calmness generates a feeling that all is well, that the adults have things under their control. It helps children to feel secure and so helps them to show some self-control. It eases their panic and soothes their aggression. It is not easy and there will be times when you are only pretending to be calm, but by doing this you are playing a huge part in maintaining positive behaviour in your setting. Even something as basic as dealing with a wasp in the room can be a chance for you to remain calm on the surface, whatever you are really feeling, so that the children learn that problems can be dealt with and their world can become safe again.

Responding to emotional outbursts within the setting

How will you react if one of the adults in your setting 'loses it' or doesn't behave with emotional balance and self-control? This can be a difficult situation. The children may be distressed by what is happening. You don't want to lose credibility yourself. You don't want to undermine the other person's professionalism. But you do have to respond.

An adult is sad

This may be in response to a huge life event for this person. They may be crying or simply 'distant', in a world of their own.

Can you explain why to the children? Gather them together in a circle and talk about times when they have been sad. Do you remember how you felt when the hamster died? Do you remember how Annie felt when her cat was run over? Talk about how they felt at such times, and then explain 'Well, that is how Sandi is feeling today.'

> **TOP TIP!**
>
> *Children need to know that it is OK to have a range of emotions from happy to sad, angry to upset. They also need to know that it is acceptable to show them in some circumstances, and that others will respect those feelings and accommodate them.*

Use such incidents as learning opportunities. This is a chance for them to show understanding and compassion, copying the example of the adults around them.

An adult displays anger towards a child

This is not acceptable behaviour and the response has to demonstrate this clearly to all concerned. The first thing is to remove the adult from the situation, just as you would remove a child. A firm 'Could you come over here,' may be sufficient. The line manager should talk to the adult later, privately, following up as appropriate, according to your own setting's professional guidelines.

At the same time another adult should deal with the child, finding out what had happened, and responding to his emotional needs – whether tears or anxiety. Encourage the other children who may have witnessed this to carry on with their activities.

When things are calm again the adult should apologise to the child and explain what had made them angry, but admitting that they should have controlled their anger. If the adult can demonstrate how to apologise in a good way, the child can learn how to do this.

> ### Behaviour and Self-control: Effective practice: 40–60+ months
>
> Ensure that children and adults make opportunities to listen to each other and explain their actions.

Adults argue

This may be one member of staff with another, or it may be a parent with a member of staff.

The first step is for a senior member of staff to intervene, in a cool, calm but firm manner, asking the adults to stop and to remove themselves from the children's presence. In a more private place remind them of the setting's Code of Conduct, pointing out any relevant statements.

Possible responses

A member of staff: inform them that they will be spoken to in the office later in the day.

Parent: speak to them straight away to gain a commitment from them that there will be no repetition.

Children: if they have witnessed this it may be necessary to explain to them in a quiet group session that this does happen, people do forget themselves sometimes – but that it isn't pleasant when this happens.

Raise questions with the children to encourage them to think about the effects of arguing:

How did it make you feel?

How do you think others feel when they see and hear you arguing with your friends?

Talk about what might cause people to argue and what other ways could be used to sort out a problem.

At a later time that day, a senior member of staff should find out the facts from each person separately. Then meet together to go over the facts, express disappointment at the inappropriate behaviour and ask for a commitment from both parties that the incident will not be repeated. The issue that provoked the situation should be dealt with and a resolution sought.

A child is sad or angry

The world is a big place. The child is aware of this, and also aware of his own limitations. He can be overcome by a situation that to us as adults seems mundane or of only passing importance. So when you have to deal with a child who is sad, subdued or crying, or with a child who is hitting out in anger, or screaming and kicking, you first need to stop and think. Don't just react. Of course you will restrain a child who is hurting himself or another child, but do it with a firmness that is kind. Reflect on what the child may be feeling. Find out what is happening from his perspective. Reassure him that you are there for him.

One of the most effective things you can do is to stay calm. The child needs to know that whatever is going on for him, however stressful he may find a certain situation, and however frightened or distressed he feels – the adults around him remain in control. This is a most reassuring feeling for the child and will help him to deal more quickly with his own emotions.

Reflecting on practice

Alice, aged 2.11 years

The children are playing with the dressing-up clothes in the house. Alice has a favourite hat with a big bunch of flowers in its band. She walks into the house area, to find that a new child who has just started today is wearing the hat. She tries to snatch it from the child, who resists and cries. A member of staff tells Alice she is naughty because Gemma is new and we

→

must be her friend and share our toys. Alice just tries to snatch the hat again, and when stopped again she screams, kicks and gets herself into a distraught state.

Alice's key worker steps in. Alice has a new baby sister at home – her special relationship with mummy seems threatened. She has to share things, give up her cot and see things that were once hers being used for this new person. She can't cope yet with any more new friends or sharing her precious belongings. It is all too much for this little girl.

The member of staff working in the house distracts Gemma with a different hat and gives Alice's key worker the other hat. When Alice is calm again her key worker rewards her with her favourite hat and pops it on Alice's head. She takes her along with her and works with her until Alice is ready to play with some of her other friends. On another day Alice may be ready to befriend and share with Gemma.

Consider the following:

1. Compare the reactions of the member of staff working in the house with Gemma with the reactions of Alice's key worker.

2. Knowing the whole picture helped Alice's key worker to offer the right sort of support in this situation.

3. Do you take the time to find out about the child's current situation when you speak with parents at the start or end of sessions each day?

Children are arguing

The children need to know that it is OK to have different opinions. It is OK to be cross when someone takes your toy. It is normal to like what someone else has and want to have it for yourself. But they have to learn that it is not acceptable to argue as this can lead to upset and possibly tears, it can even develop into a physical attack. So if you have to deal with children arguing or fighting, there need to be two features to your response – the first is to stop the argument and the second is to help the children find a different way to resolve their differences.

Your setting's behaviour policy will include guidelines on the ways to handle children in these circumstances. You should always remain aware of the fact that you are dealing with a child not an adult. Remember that they can't yet control their emotions – they don't have the maturity to do this automatically. They may be feeling out of control in a large world and away from their primary care-givers.

Very young children arguing over ownership of a toy can often be distracted before they resort to hitting or biting.

> *Behaviour and Self-control: Planning and resourcing: 40–60+ months*
>
> Make time to listen to children respectfully when they raise injustices, and involve them in finding a 'best fit' solution.

If the children are old enough to discuss what is happening allow each one in turn to tell you what happened. Listen carefully, have patience and let them tell you the whole story in their own words without interruptions. Then help them to find an alternative solution. Talk it through. Take as long as you need. You can end up suppressing unwanted behaviour if you rush the process or impose a solution. It is better in the long term to devote time to showing the children how to think things through and talk about their feelings rather than lashing out. In this way they will be developing their own skills and learning strategies for dealing with conflict or tricky situations – an important life skill.

In touch with parents – about the child's emotional development

You want to show parents that you will be devoting considerable time and effort to thinking about their child's emotional needs. They need to know that you have their child's emotional development at heart, as this plays a large part in developing their ability to show control and self-restraint – and so 'behave well'.

On registration

This may be the best opportunity you will get to spend a substantial amount of time talking with one set of parents. They will be keen to talk about their child. They will be thrilled that you are taking such a personal interest in him. Use the time well.

To find out about the child's emotional development start by asking about the child's preferences:

What makes their child happy?

What distresses him?

What is he afraid of?

How does their child show these feelings? What should you be looking for?

For each of these find out how the parents usually respond:

> What do they do and what words do they use to reassure the child?

Self-care: Effective practice: 8–20 months

Talk to parents about how their baby communicates needs. Ensure that parents and carers who speak languages other than English are able to share their views.

You will have to make a quick judgement on whether these methods fit in with nursery practice. Talk with the parents about what you would usually do in any of these situations. Would they find this acceptable? Explain why you have certain policies for dealing with children who are sad, or frightened and so on, and point out where these are written up in your brochure and your behaviour policy. This is the time when you can find a compromise if you have to.

When there's been an upset

It should be policy that whenever a child has been distressed or very angry you tell parents about it. The timing of this was discussed in more detail in Chapter 3. It is much better if you give this information without being prompted. It should be a routine procedure. The child may remember the incident later and may not be able to explain it well to their parents. By the time the parents are able to see you the next day they can have built this up in their minds into a more serious event than it possibly was.

Talk to the parents about the event, what caused it, what actually happened, how their child responded, and any actions you took. If your actions were particularly successful in calming the child, point this out to the parents. It might be a strategy they could use at home. If they suggested the approach to you at the registration meeting make sure you let them know how well it worked and thank them for telling you about it. As in all aspects of the child's time with you, you want this to be a positive relationship – the parents, yourself and the child working together to promote the child's emotional competence.

Conclusion

This chapter has explained how children gradually acquire a range of emotions, and that it is necessary for you to recognise the stage of any child's emotional development so that you can support them in dealing with the highs and the lows of their lives in appropriate ways. By responding in ways that the child can understand and can relate to, you will be supporting and encouraging their ongoing emotional development at the same time as you are helping them to solve today's problem. You now also have some practical ideas for helping children to talk about emotions that will impact on their ability to explain their own feelings when they need to.

Key ideas summary

You now have an understanding of:

- How to recognise children's emotional states.
- How to measure a child's emotional maturity.
- How to help children develop their emotional vocabulary and understanding.
- Your role in supporting the children's emotional development.
- How to deal with emotional outbursts in the setting.

Going further

Many of the familiar books on child development give little space or time to identifying and tracking the way that children develop emotionally. If you want to investigate this aspect of child development further you will need to look for books in the psychology sections of book shops and libraries. Some useful titles are listed in the references. Two titles that are particularly good starting points are:

Schaffer, H.R. (2004) *Introducing Child Psychology,* Oxford: Blackwell Publishing.

Smith, P., Cowie, H. and Black, M. (2003, 4th edn) *Understanding Children's Development,* Oxford: Blackwell Publishing.

Squirrel says

Squirrel was washing a window when he noticed Violet Vole coming home alone from school. All of the other children were already home. He wondered why Violet was so late. She was walking very slowly. Perhaps that was why she was late. She sat on the bench, swinging her legs, which were too short to reach the floor when she sat down. Her hands were in her pockets. Her head was down.

'That is one sad child,' said Squirrel to himself. 'I wonder what can be troubling her?'

He finished polishing his window. Violet was still sitting on the bench. He decided to go and find out if she was all right.

Violet didn't even look up when he sat down beside her on the bench.

'You look sad, Violet,' said Squirrel. 'Would you like to tell me what the matter is?'

Violet said something. She said it so quietly that Squirrel couldn't work out what she'd said.

'You'll have to speak up a bit, my dear.' said Squirrel in a kind voice.

'I've no one to play with,' said Violet. 'My best friend Daisy has moved house. And I bet she has loads of new friends now. And I've got no one.'

'Did you tell the others – did you tell Fran and Ramsay and all the others that I've just seen walking home together?'

'No. 'Cos they're bigger than me and they won't want to be my friend.'

'Well let's find out, shall we?' said Squirrel, taking Violet's hand and setting off for the door to Warren Buildings.

The others had been home, changed into their play clothes and were just coming out again to play. Squirrel explained to them, 'Violet is feeling sad, and she needs some friends to play, because her best friend has moved away.'

'She can play with us,' said the other children. 'We could always do with another person for our football team. Go and tell your mum, Violet, and then come and join us. Be quick!'

Squirrel says,

'Let other people know when you are sad or lonely and then they'll be able to help you.'

Chapter 6

Develop self-esteem and personal pride

What this chapter will explore:

- Helping children to become aware of themselves as individuals
- Helping children to recognise their own achievements
- Helping children to know that they are valued

This chapter explores how the child develops an awareness that he is special, and that he has an important part to play. When a child has this strong sense of self-esteem it means that he doesn't need to seek attention in anti-social ways, so it is a quality that you want to encourage and to work towards.

Self-esteem is how the child evaluates himself as a person. It can be high or low dependent on the view he takes of himself and his abilities. But before the child can evaluate himself he has to know that he is an individual, separate from all other people. Then he must be conscious of who he is, what he looks like and what he can do. It is only at this stage that he can place a value on himself. Self-esteem refers to the way in which the child evaluates himself. It indicates:

'The extent to which the individual believes himself to be capable, significant, successful and worthy.'

(Coopersmith, 1967, cited in Schaffer, 2004, p 311)

Developing self-awareness

Because the new-born baby doesn't see himself as separate from the mother he isn't aware of himself as 'a person'. The change to self-awareness comes at about 18 months of age. At this age, researchers found that if they put a spot of rouge on a child's nose and showed him his reflection he touched his own nose. Before this age, the child may have been amused by the reflection, but was unaffected by the spot of rouge (Lewis and Brooks-Gunn, 1979).

Once the child knows he is an individual he can start to build his own self-image. Your focus should be on making sure that the image of himself that the child acquires is a positive one; that he learns about his importance to you; that he experiences positive feedback when he tries out new skills and attempts new and challenging experiences; and that his thoughts and feelings are worth having and sharing.

Developing a self-concept

A child's concept of self is a reference to the image that children build of themselves. They start by being able to describe what they look like (based on Schaffer, 2004):

'I am a boy.'

'My hair is brown.'

And the sort of things they own:

'I have a bike.'

'I've got a cat.'

They then start to describe their capabilities:

'I can run really fast.'

'I can get my own drink.'

And by the time they go to school they include descriptions of their psychological traits:

'I'm scared in the dark.'

'I'm really happy when we go to play in the park.'

> ### Self-confidence and Self-esteem: Look, listen and note: 40–60+ months
>
> Children's pleasure in who they are and what they can do.

Research has been carried out to find out how children understand other people. One well-documented piece of research was carried out by Livesley and Bromley (1973), when they asked children to describe other people. The youngest children in their research group were 7 year olds, the oldest were 15. The older children introduced information about a person's thoughts, feelings and attributes, whereas the younger children described people purely on their physical appearance. This was despite the fact that they had been asked to concentrate on what sort of person the individual was, not on their appearance. Later research disputed this apparent lack of ability in the younger children, and criticised the research methods for inhibiting the children. However, opinion remains that children do develop from taking an external view of people to taking an internal view of them.

> ### Understanding self
> The concept of self develops through the following stages:
>
> The child views himself as an entity with the mother.
>
> The child sees himself as a separate person.
>
> The child can describe himself by what he looks like and what he owns.
>
> The child can describe himself in terms of what he can do.
>
> The child can describe his psychological traits.
>
> The child can compare himself with others, in gradually more complex ways.
>
> The child can describe his weaknesses as well as his strengths.
>
> The child is aware that other people have internal feelings, thoughts and ideologies that may be different from his own.

Some activities to help children recognise their own self

These will be part of your PSE programme, but also fit well into some aspects of Physical Development (PD) as well as providing children with a chance to practise counting as part of their Problem Solving, Reasoning and Number (PSRN) work.

> *Self-confidence and Self-esteem: Development matters:*
> *30–50 months*
>
> Have a sense of personal identity.

> *Self-confidence and Self-esteem: Development matters:*
> *40–60+ months*
>
> Have an awareness and pride of self as having own identity and abilities.

Create pictograms or sets

Prepare some pictures of the chosen items for children to choose and place in the right column or set. Try:

My favourite fruit is ... apple/banana/orange.

I have 0/1/2 or more sisters/brothers.

I have straight/curly hair.

I have white/brown/red/blue shoes.

Play 'Musical Me'

Mark out a space, or have an adult standing in a strategic spot.

Play the music, children dance around.

When the music stops the adult calls out, e.g., 'Anyone wearing red' or 'Anyone who can climb to the top of the climbing frame'.

Those who match the criteria go to the adult and the others sit down where they are.

Count how many are standing up. Or how many are sitting down.

Tell the children: '11 children can climb to the top of the climbing frame'.

Start the music and play again.

Write a poem/riddle about yourself

Show the children a simple poem format and explain what the process is, for example:

I am a girl with long golden hair. *(What I look like)*

I like to walk in the woods. *(Something I like to do)*

I am quite brave. *(The sort of person I am)*

Who am I? *(Goldilocks)*

Or:

I am covered in fur.

I have very big teeth.

I am fierce.

Who am I? *(The wolf in Red Riding Hood)*

Write one together about a character from a well-known story, or about you if you are brave enough! As the old joke goes: the teacher brings in her new hat, the one that she wore to a wedding recently, and places it on a table at the front of the classroom. She asks the children to write a description of it. A child raises her hand and asks – 'How do you spell "horrible"?'

Children can now work on their own versions. You could display these with photos or paintings of the children or characters described in the poems.

At the end of the day

Before the children go home you can spend a few minutes thinking about all the things that happened during the day.

Can you tell me something that made me/Joe/Suzie sad today?

Who can do something now that they couldn't do yesterday? What is it?

Tell me about something that you have learnt today.

Who can tell us about someone who did something kind/helpful/thoughtful today?

Can you remind us of something that made us laugh today?

TOP TIP!

Make sure that you end on a positive note. You could always finish with a clap or high-fives all round. This is the emotion that your children will leave with. If it is a positive emotion this will help them to go out of the door with a sense of their own success, and optimistic about life.

Developing self-esteem

Now that he knows that he is a person in his own right, and that he has his own appearance, abilities and preferences, the child will start to judge himself. He will do this by comparing himself with others, and by taking on board the comments made by others about him.

> *'A deep, loving human connection in early life is at the very core of self-esteem.'*

> (Sunderland, 2003, p 15)

Dispositions and Attitudes: Effective practice: 16–26 months

Ensure that each child is recognised as a valuable contributor to the group and celebrate cultural, religious and ethnic experiences.

Things you can do to show a child that you value him

● Look deep into the child's face when you are listening to him – let the child see that you are pleased to be with him. Get down to the child's level when you are talking with him. A lack of eye contact and positive facial expressions, especially to a younger child, can result in him feeling as if he doesn't count and eventually he can switch off, and stop engaging with you. (See Reflecting on practice box on page 123.)

● Some research was carried out to find out how practitioners interpreted children's behaviour (Degotardi and Davis, 2008). The researchers asked the practitioners to interpret the child's behaviour on two separate occasions, once when the children were playing and again when they were receiving care (for example nappy changing). When the children were observed playing the practitioners used professional terms in their feedback to the researchers to describe what the children were doing. When the practitioners were giving care, they only described the adult's actions. They didn't interpret the child's behaviour or response to the care they were receiving. Yet, as the researchers say, 'routine times provide infant and ECP [Early Childhood Practitioner] with valuable developmental and relationship-building opportunities'. (See the Top Tip! on page 124.)

● When children show you a piece of independent work of which they are obviously proud, respond with equal pleasure. This isn't the time to remind the child of the things he could have done, should have added, or might have taken more care over. This is the child's spontaneous work, he has completed his own plan, he feels that it is good and he wants to share that pleasure and pride with you. Talk with the child about what he has done, and ask him how he did it. He is sharing something of himself with you, so thank him, praise him and appreciate his effort. Children know when you are paying lip-service and just saying the word 'thanks'. You have to mean it, you have to be interested.

Reflecting on practice

The student in the room

It is a Key Stage 1 classroom. At the start of the day the teacher is sitting on a chair with the children gathered around her as she takes the register. The new student teacher comes in, finds an adult-sized chair, carries it to the front of the group and sits on it next to the teacher. She folds her arms and then rests them on her knees so that her body is hunched over.

Her first task of the day is to help a group of children with their story writing. The children are sitting round a typical classroom table, on their child-sized chairs. The student stands behind one of the children, with her arms folded. She says nothing. The children have a problem, and one of them goes over to the teacher and asks her for help.

In the afternoon a 17-year-old student from a nearby school comes in on work experience. She is asked to supervise a group of children who are making puppets. She gets a chair – child-sized – and sits at the table with the children. She asks them what they are doing, they tell her in excited tones; she helps them find the resources they need and she assists with cutting. The group is vibrant and productive.

Consider the following:

1. How was the body language of these two girls interpreted by the children?
2. What messages did the children get?
3. Think about your own body language. What messages are your children reading into the way you stand or sit?

TOP TIP!

If a child has soiled himself in some way – perhaps he has used his nappy, been sick or spilt food on himself – it's possible that he may feel some level of emotional distress as well as the more obvious physical discomfort. When you clean him up, you are sorting out and removing the physical discomfort but you should be aware that you are also easing the emotional distress.

When you do this you are showing him that he doesn't have to face things on his own, and that when uncomfortable things happen they can be sorted out. You show him that someone is there to help him. It may not be the most pleasant task for you but remember that you aren't just clearing up the mess, you are shaping the child's view of the world as a place where he can survive the unpleasant things that will happen to him.

Not Now, Bernard (McKee, 1996) is a story that is often read to young children. No matter what Bernard tells his parents they are always too busy with their own adult lives to take notice. Eventually the monster that he's been telling them about eats Bernard and takes his place in the family home. And still nobody notices.

Recognising achievement

It seems obvious that if children are to develop a sense of pride in their own achievements they must first of all be able to recognise what their achievements are. But do they?

Record keeping is important to you as a professional because it is the way for you to remember what the child can already do, what he is learning to do, and what he needs to do next. It is also a useful and practical way to help the children track their own achievements.

Why not try this?

I can ...

Have a selection of outline drawings. Think of the ones you would get in a child's colouring book. Within some of the parts write simple phrases to complete the sentence 'I can ...', for example:

➜

hop

skip

jump

balance on one leg

Children colour each section in as they achieve. When they have finished the sheet they can take it home. Add a code or a reference number in the corner so that the dates when it is started and completed can be recorded in your own records against that code.

These could be pre-written statements of achievement, or you could tailor the sheet to an individual child, for example, George needs encouragement to dress/undress, so you create a sheet for him that includes

'I can ...'

put my shoes on

fasten Velcro®

hang my coat up

pull up the zip on my coat

Now I can ...

Have some laminated notices near the different activities. Use one statement per notice, such as:

'Now I can count to 10.'

'Now I can name all of these shapes.'

Leave room underneath the heading to write down the names of the children who have achieved this, this week.

Change the notices each week or add some new ones so that there is always a challenge for every child (see www.pearsoned.co.uk/essentialguides for some examples).

Self-confidence and Self-esteem: Planning and resourcing: 22–36 months

Record individual achievements that reflect significant progress for every child: one may have stepped on the slide, another may be starting to play readily with others.

Rewarding achievement or effort

> **TOP TIP!**
>
> *There are stickers that you can buy with all sorts of messages written or depicted on them.*
>
> *A cheaper option is to use the little sticky circles that you can buy in many high street shops. You are more likely to hand out these cheap stickers than the more expensive variety.*

Stickers are always popular for rewarding achievement and effort. Having a sticker serves several purposes:

- It reminds the child that he has done something well as he gets on with the rest of the day.

- It is a prompt to the parent that the child has done something well and they can ask him about it when they collect him.

- It shows the other children that he has done something well.

> **Reflecting on practice**
>
> Occasionally you will need to address unwanted behaviour in a particular child, but you can still use your stickers for this.
>
> Have a laminated board or white board with a smiley face on it, placed up high so that the children can't reach it, but so that it is in sight of the child. Attach a small note explaining the behaviour you are looking for: 'Mark is trying to use a quiet voice instead of calling out'.
>
> Every time you see him speaking quietly or getting on without making a fuss you put a sticker on the board. You don't need to tell him – whatever you do, don't call out in a loud voice! If he notices you, do a simple thumbs-up sign. He will look at the board and he will be aware of his increasing number of stickers.
>
> If you see him, or hear him calling out inappropriately, peel a sticker off. Again, don't say anything.
>
> At the end of the session help him to count up his stickers. You will have planned his reward at the start of the day: 'If you get ten stickers you will sit on the big chair at story time. If you have more than ten stickers you will choose a friend to sit on the chair with you at story time.' There is no punishment for not getting ten stickers, or whatever number you have decided is achievable in a session. He starts the next session with a clean board. →

Consider the following:

This is a discreet way to tackle the unwanted behaviour while still maintaining the child's self-esteem. It rewards the efforts that he is making to address his behaviour.

There will be occasions when you have to deal with children whose behaviour is causing a lot of disruption. Clearly you have to tackle this, but at this young age you have to be conscious of the need to build, not destroy a child's self-esteem. If the child is faced with a barrage of 'no' and 'stop' all day it can have a negative influence, just when you want to affect the child in positive ways. You don't want to end up with a child who thinks that everything they do is wrong, or bad. To succeed you have to find a way to reward the efforts the child does make to behave in appropriate ways. The example below explains what Chloe's teacher did (further material on this is also available at www.pearsoned.co.uk/essentialguides).

Reflecting on practice

Chloe, aged 5.8 years

Chloe has many difficulties with her behaviour and her school is trying to get additional help for her but need evidence of the problems she has coping in a classroom.

Her teacher has identified several areas for improvement:

- Chloe needs to stay in her place when asked to.
- Chloe needs to finish any task she is given.
- Chloe needs to stop interfering and disturbing the others at her table.

If all of these issues are addressed in every activity/work session Chloe could start to feel either special because she gets lots of attention for this behaviour, or victimised because the teacher is always telling her off. But the behaviour can't be ignored.

It's difficult to prove your case to an outside body when you can only say things such as, 'She's always getting up', 'She never stays in her seat', etc. What you need is evidence. On a piece of paper Chloe's teacher wrote out steps towards Chloe's target behaviour for insertion in an exercise book. She wrote these in child-friendly words, and did it with Chloe present. The first steps were:

For three minutes Chloe has to:

- stay in her seat;
- and finish her work;
- and not talk to the other children.

$\rightarrow$

The words are well spaced down the page so that they fill the page. The paper is taped to the inside cover of the exercise book across the top. On the opposite page Chloe's teacher has divided the page lengthways into the number of sessions in the day when this particular behaviour will be expected. In this instance, three.

During each session Chloe could earn three stickers, one for each step. Over the day she could achieve nine stickers.

At the end of the day the teacher can see how well Chloe did by the number of stickers – and by the number of empty spaces. Chloe, however, will only register all the times when she did well and was rewarded.

On day two, the teacher simply tucks the used page of the book under the loose list of steps, so that the new page is ready, and she can still read the steps.

Consider the following:

Here are some of the positive ways this approach can be of benefit. You may be able to think of more.

1. The teacher can check the results against her lesson plans to see which activities lead to success, and when and with what type of activity Chloe struggled to behave.
2. The teacher has the information that will help her to plan for more success.
3. The teacher has the information to share with the SENCO.
4. Chloe's parents can see where Chloe succeeds and where she has problems.
5. Chloe will benefit from the focused support while maintaining her self-esteem.

Use of language

The child who has low self-esteem may internalise any critical things said to him, until they become his own view of himself. Words that might have been said in anger, or words that were simply one person's opinion, can stay with the child. He may go over and over them in his mind until they seem far worse than was ever the intention of the person who said those things. It can reach a point where the child believes those things to be the truth about him (Sunderland, 2003).

This may be an extreme case. Such children may have low self-esteem because of the situation at home. But it is certainly worth keeping this thought with you, and following the old adage of 'think before you speak'.

Why not try this?

The little baby takes his first step without anyone holding him. What happens? He is praised, cuddled, clapped. Everyone smiles and gives the baby loads of positive vibes. 'Again!' the parent exhorts the child. The child does it again, and gets all the praise again. A phone call is made to let granny know. A video clip is made on the phone and sent to daddy.

The three year old builds a tower of bricks higher than he has ever managed before. He looks to the adult for praise and adulation. What does he get?

'Well done. Now tidy it all away.'

'Be careful, that might topple over and hurt someone.'

If you are allowed time to observe your colleagues try making a note of everyone's reactions to children's achievements. Don't, however, tell your colleagues what you are looking at in case that affects their responses to the children. Don't record who said what, just the words that are used and the gender and age of the recipient. For example:

M. 3 yr – 'That's brilliant. Did you do it all by yourself?'

F. 2.5 yr – 'What a lovely pink painting. Shall we put it somewhere to dry?'

F. 4yr – 'Yes, you have finished it, but you haven't kept inside the lines, have you?'

Analyse your findings to find out the sort of responses children get.

- Does it differ for boys and girls?
- Does it depend on the age of the child or their ability?
- Does anyone ask the child how he did it, or if he is pleased with it?
- Which statements or responses will boost the child's self-esteem?

Look for opportunities to reinforce self-esteem

Self-esteem is a fragile thing. Try to reinforce it as much, and as often, as you can.

Choices and consequences

This is a way to discipline a child according to Daniel Hughes (2006) so that you can help the child to learn to be a sociable person without damaging his self-esteem. He suggests that you should respond to a child who misbehaves by telling him that his choice of action wasn't a good one, and that there are other choices he could have made; or by telling him of the consequences of the choice that he made. For example:

- Ben, aged 4, bites Millie, aged 3 because she won't give him the big car.

  You could say, 'Ben, that wasn't a good choice you made then. Let's think about some other choices you could have made that won't get you into trouble or hurt someone else. You may be cross but you can still make a good choice.'

- Barry, aged 5, is sitting under the table and refusing to come out and join in with the others who are going outside to use the big toys.

  You say, 'Barry, you need to come out from under the table.'

  He replies, 'No.'

  You tell him, 'Well that is your choice, but the consequence is that you will miss out on choosing which bike you have. Still, that's your choice at the moment. I'll be here doing this job, and when you are ready to go out and join in you can let me know and I'll take you outside with the others.'

> ### Self-care: Look, listen and note: 22–36 months
>
> What children choose to do when presented with several options.

Six for one

Sue Jenner, who devised and wrote *The Parent/Child Game* (1999), says that for every criticism a child gets he should have six statements of praise. This will help the child to maintain his self-esteem. This may seem an extreme position to take, but the principle of trying to praise more often than you criticise is worth aiming for.

Change negative to positive

Children need you to show them how they can face what life has to offer, and overcome the negative parts. By taking a more optimistic view of things children will start to develop resilience and pride.

- The pessimist sees failure as a permanent state: 'I never get anything right', 'I always get things wrong'.

- The optimist sees failure as a chance to learn: 'I can't do that yet', 'I should be better at that if I have another go at it tomorrow when I'm feeling less tired'.

Reflecting on practice

Robert, 4.3 years

Robert has had a very troubled start to life. His mother is very young, and single, and she has had a number of boyfriends who have distracted her from Robert's care. After a lot of intervention and support from Social Services things are improving at home. However, the experience has left Robert feeling that he doesn't count, that he can be set aside in favour of others.

On Thursday morning the children were making masks. Robert daubed glue on Mary's mask and upset her. He hid the gold ribbons that were the favourite 'hair' decoration. He finished his own mask eventually. 'That's great', said his key worker, Maddie. 'It's not' said Robert. 'I love the way that you made the hair from those wood shavings', said Maddie. Robert took hold of his mask and ripped it before throwing it in the bin.

Robert's actions were typical of the child with low self-esteem:

● He damaged other children's work.

● He took away and hid things that other people valued.

● He destroyed his own possessions when they were admired.

● He is taking control of the situation and causing the effects that he expects to happen to him, even though he doesn't like those effects. He rubbishes himself before others can rubbish him.

● He spoils things for others in the way that things have always been spoilt for him.

In other words, he is getting in there first – you can't hurt me because I've already hurt myself.

The approach Maddie is taking is one that will be a long, slow process, but it is the only way to help this little boy retrieve a sense of his own value and worth.

● She continues to give him praise, even though he rejects it.

● She gives praise for every tiny good thing he does.

● She gives him lots of encouragement for each small step towards achieving something – work or behaviour.

● She maintains the boundaries. She doesn't let him get away with breaking those rules that keep him and the others safe and happy. This helps him to feel safe and secure.

● She provides stability.

● She is very patient with him, never losing her temper however far he pushes her.

● She is sensitive to his situation at home.

→

Consider the following:

1. Are there any other steps that you would advise Maddie to take in her dealings with Robert?
2. Is there anything that her line manager could do to support her?
3. What would you do about the mask? Think about the end of the session when everyone else has a mask to take home.

Useful words to promote self-esteem – or not such useful words

Do you ever think about the actual words you use when you are interacting with the children? There are many expressions in common usage that could be expressed in more positive ways.

Why not try this?

Look through this list and mark the statements that you think will help to promote self-esteem.

Remember the rule about using scissors.

Stop looking out of the window.

Please look this way.

Stop messing about in the line.

I don't think I've ever seen such a smart group as this.

I need to choose someone to feed the fish and it's hard to choose as you're all sitting so well.

Don't wave those scissors around.

Let's make a really straight line today.

Thank you for sitting so quietly ready for the story.

No you can't go outside yet. You haven't finished that tidying up.

You are so quick at tidying up I guess you'll be going out in half a minute.

I'm looking for someone sensible to take this message – Dan, you are sensible, you can take it.

I can see some great work going on in the sand.

Remember to hang your coats up when you get in.

Don't forget to hang your coats up.

I don't want to see the mess I saw this morning.

I'm spoilt for choice – you are all so sensible, but I can only choose one. So today I shall choose ... Dan.

Record keeping

You can help the children to take a more optimistic view by the words that you use in your record keeping. Use the following three headings to grade your children's achievements, especially for records that will be seen by the parent and/or the child. These words help to put learning into a context of ambition and expectation of success, rather than a critical opinion of what the child 'can't do'.

I can do this really well.

I can do this but need some more practice/I still need some help to do this.

I can't do this yet.

Marking work

When you mark children's work you have a superb chance to build up the child's view of himself as an achiever. At this age he is probably doing his best. There will come a time when children present poor work because they didn't listen or didn't allow themselves enough time, but, generally speaking, children want to achieve, they want to please the adults because they like the praise.

So marking work should be seen as a chance to find out what he can do well, what he needs to practise and what he still needs help with. It is not a time to ridicule or belittle a child.

TOP TIP!

When children reach the stage where you are marking a piece of work there are two points that you should always take into account:

1. *Are you marking the work in a written form for your own benefit so that you can keep track of their achievements and their learning needs, or so that parents can see what the child has achieved when they look through the books? In other words, are you writing for adults?*

2. *Are you writing down something that the child will read and, maybe, will read on his own, without a chance to ask for added details of what it means, or what the words actually say?*

Know your audience, and match the words and the comments to that audience.

Be precise in what you are marking. It should match what you were teaching. Remember your learning objective, and mark that. For example:

Learning objective: CLL: Writing: ELG: Attempt writing for different purposes ... such as lists.

Activity: Write a list of all the things you want to take on your picnic.

Marking/Assessment: Did the child create a list with the items written one under the other? Yes. Objective achieved.

If you try to mark everything, every time, the child will start to lose faith in his abilities, and his self-esteem will take a knock. It's like playing a game where he doesn't know all of the rules. Or Sam thinks he knows the rules. 'You are to write a list of things that you'll take on a picnic', but after you've marked it he discovers that he was also supposed to spell everything correctly, write neatly, keep his letters the right way round, not cross anything out, and so on, and nobody told him about these rules. He was feeling proud of what he'd done. He had a really long list and it looked like the list you'd shown him. Now he just feels dejected because of all of the things he's done wrong.

- 'Good': this means absolutely nothing when you come to check his books at the end of the year. It is meaningless to the parents, who won't necessarily know what the task was. Sam won't know whether you are pleased with the contents of his list, the length of his list, his hand writing ...

- 'You kept all your words underneath each other and made a great list. Well done, Sam': this explains the nature of the task, and what he did that was right. And it lets Sam know that you appreciate his effort. You will remember the task and be able to keep your records of Sam's achievements accurately. Sam's parents will understand the task when he shows them his work.

Marking is best done in the presence of the child. Use it as a time to engage in a discussion with the child. Let them tell you about their work. Add notes about this additional information if it is pertinent to the learning objective. Ask interested questions that allow the child to expand on their knowledge. All of this will demonstrate to the child that you are interested in him and in his achievements and thoughts. It all builds his self-esteem as a learner.

Dispositions and Attitudes: Planning and resourcing: 22–36 months

As children differ in their degree of self-assurance, plan to convey to each child that you appreciate them and their efforts.

Developing a professional Code of Conduct within the setting

The attitude of the staff in any setting is going to play a large part in maintaining, or even building, a child's self-esteem. Your words and actions, and the way that you respond to children will have a huge impact on them. They need to feel accepted, valued, happy and confident. You need to show tolerance, patience, diplomacy and sensitivity. To do this you have to be aware of your own level of self-esteem.

You meet up with your friend, and you notice that she's wearing a new top. You could say something like, 'I love that top', or you can say, 'That top looks great with those trousers. You are good at putting things together.' This second comment reflects on her ability to choose, her taste and her decision making. The first one only commented on the top, not on the person. The effect on your friend is that the second comment would boost her self-esteem. Taking this principle into the workplace, look out for occasions when you can praise a colleague's decision or planning in a way that will boost her self-esteem.

> 'That's a great display. How did you manage to fix that in place? Can you show me how you did it?'

> 'I noticed that the children looked really engrossed when they were with you in the garden area.'

> 'You have a knack with getting Pete to settle down. Can you explain what you do in case I ever have to receive him one morning?'

If this was the way that all members of your staff spoke to each other, you would soon have a team of confident professionals who would in turn inspire confidence in the children and the parents.

Look for ways to praise your colleagues as well as praising the children.

In touch with parents – helping parents to settle their children in

There will be countless permutations of emotional conditions experienced by the parents/children starting at your setting. There will be the shy, the exuberant, the 'old hands', the familiar, the reluctant and the excited. The nature of the parent might be very different from the nature of the child. In each case you have to be able to settle the child with the minimum of distress.

There will be a system already set up for introducing the child and the parent to the setting. This will be explained during the induction meeting, when you can find out any anxieties the parents may have about this particular child. Their expectations and their knowledge of the child will inform you of any potential difficulties. Discuss with them:

How often will they attend?

Will the parent stay?

What is a good way for the parent to leave?

Can you contact the parent later to let them know how the child is settling in?

What will happen if the child doesn't settle?

Self-confidence and Self-esteem: Effective practice: 30–50 months

Create positive relationships with parents by listening to them and offering information and support.

Some children will find it more difficult to settle. Have some strategies ready to use:

The shy child: Suggest to the parents that they let the child bring a toy from home. He can show his key worker how it works, what it does, what is the right way to play with it. In this way he can become familiar with the setting and the children all around him, with the comfort of the familiar. Many children just need time to adapt. Given kind support and understanding they will eventually warm up to the routines and resources and play a full part in the setting.

The quiet child: He may like a buddy. Choose another child to accompany him. Don't choose the over-confident one with loads of friends as he may overwhelm this child. Choose someone who will be able to 'Show Nicky where the car mat is' or 'Nicky loves doing puzzles. Can you show him some of ours? Perhaps you can do that new one together.' Find out from the parent what he specially likes doing so that you can suggest an activity that you know he'll enjoy.

The clingy child: Once the induction period is over and you expect the children to stay for the full session without the parent, you may still have some children who may fight to stay with the parent, or to make the parent stay with them. This needs a firm but quiet response from staff. Tell the parent what you will do in these cases so that they can support you.

There are some children who are distressed by the actual act of parting from the parent. In these instances there are two options:

1. It can be a long drawn-out separation time.

2. It can be over fairly quickly.

Some parents drag the parting out because they actually feel good about themselves in this situation – my child can't bear to be without me! You have to talk sensitively with them about this, explaining that their child is distressed by the act of parting, not by being apart. Once the parent has gone most children can be encouraged to take part in activities and they play well throughout the session. By dragging out the leaving time these parents are putting their child through ten minutes, maybe half-an-hour of distress when it could have been over in two minutes.

Suggest a different approach: 'We are here. We are going to hang your coat up. We are going to find you something to do.' This could be agreed between parent and child on the journey to the setting. Some children are better being told what they are going to do in this instance. 'When we get to nursery we will say hello to Emma, then we will hang your coat up and find you an apron so that you can paint. It'll be dry by the time I come back for you, so we can bring it home and stick it up in the kitchen. I wonder if granny will like it when she comes tomorrow?'

TOP TIP!

If this clinging continues some parents may find the answer is to ask someone else to take the child to the setting – a family member or even another child's parent. 'Today Sasha and her mum are taking you.' After a few days of success at this, you can be the one to collect Sasha. Having another child with them may be the answer for some children.

If parents can be helped to see that their child isn't 'odd' or 'not as good as the others' you can take away their potential to respond to the child with anger, or shame. If you know what to do, then obviously you have met children like this before – therefore their child is just like them. If parents respond with anger and shame this is destructive to the child's sense of worth, he will feel that he has let them down, that they don't understand his fears, that he is not worth understanding. It is a negative cycle of emotional upset that is best avoided, and damaging to the child's self-esteem.

Self-confidence and Self-esteem: Planning and resourcing: 22–36 months

Seek and exchange information with parents about young children's concerns, so that they can be reassured if they feel uncertain.

After a few visits, when you feel that the child should be settling in well, observe the children as they arrive. The child who has a high sense of self-esteem should be displaying the following behaviour:

When the child arrives he:

– is chatty;

– is happy to leave the parent;

– looks pleased to see other children and staff;

– talks to other children and staff;

– finds an activity that he wants to do;

– allows or encourages other children to play with him;

– focuses on what he is doing;

– is willing to show and tell.

Conclusion

This chapter has shown you how you can build and maintain a child's self-esteem so that he feels valued. You will be affecting a child's self-esteem by the way that you speak to him, the way that you respond to his behaviour and to the efforts that he makes to learn, play and socialise. Your behaviour towards him will help to create his self-image and then the way that he evaluates the person that he believes himself to be.

Key ideas summary

You now have an understanding that if children are to have a high level of self-esteem, you must:

● Help the children to see themselves as special individuals.

● Help the children to recognise their own achievements.

● Show the children that you value them.

● Give positive feedback to the efforts they make.

● Act in a tolerant and patient way.

● Speak to them in positive ways.

Going further

An Internet search of 'self-esteem in young children' will bring you a wealth of material, from book titles to advice for parents.

Sage Publishers and Speechmark Publishing offer many books on this subject.

Squirrel says

Squirrel loved reading. His favourite books were adventure stories. Every Thursday afternoon he went to the library in the high street and chose two books. Today he'd chosen *Sam's Seaside Adventure* and *Danger in the Woods*. He was going to read *Danger in the Woods* first; there was a picture of a girl in a red cloak on the cover, and something with a long nose hiding behind a tree. He was just settling down in his brown leather armchair when he thought he heard a noise. He stopped and listened. There it was again. A very quiet noise at his door. Someone very small or very shy must have knocked. He got up and went to see who it could be. It was Grandpa Mouse from number 3.

'Hello there, Mr Mouse,' said Squirrel. 'How can I help you?'

'Er, excuse me, Squirrel,' said Mr Mouse in such a teeny-tiny voice that Squirrel could hardly hear him.

'Er, I was wondering – um – well, I was hoping – um …'

'Yes, Mr Mouse. What can I do for you?'

Mr Mouse put his paw into the pocket of his jacket and pulled out a brown envelope, with **Mr G. Mouse, 3 Warren Buildings**, written on it.

'It's a letter,' said Mr Mouse

'I can see that,' said Squirrel.

'Well, er, can you tell me what it says, please?' asked Mr Mouse.

'Oh, you want me to read it for you!'

'Yes, please. You see, I'm not very good at reading small things now. It's my eyes you know,' said Mr Mouse, pointing to his thick round glasses.

'No problem. Come in. Sit down – ooh, not there. That chair's got a rickety old leg and will likely tip you off! I should fix it but I don't know how to do it.'

➜

'Let me do it,' said Mr Mouse. 'I'm good at mending things and I'd like to help you.'

'Well, that's brilliant,' said Squirrel. 'We'll be able to help each other.

Squirrel says,

'Everyone's good at something. Do you know what your friend is good at?'

Learn how to behave so that learning can take place

What this chapter will explore:

Creating the atmosphere:

- How the staff can set a standard of social behaviour
- How the staff can help the children to work and play by the rules
- The way that children speak to each other and to adults

Behaviour for learning:

- The processes that are involved in learning
- The effect of the brain's development on children's ability to learn
- Helping children to pay attention
- Ideas for encouraging concentration

This chapter concentrates on the behaviour that has to occur if the children are going to be able to learn. There are two aspects to this. The first is to look at the behaviour that creates the atmosphere which will encourage and promote learning. The second is to consider the particular patterns of behaviour that the child has to exhibit if he is to learn.

Behaviour to create the atmosphere that promotes learning

In Chapter 1 the issue of boundary setting was examined. One boundary that was identified, but not dealt with at that point, was the boundary that enables play and learning to take place. This boundary includes all the actions that you take to manage the day-to-day organisation of activities and interactions within your setting. It includes social conventions that might be loosely termed 'good manners' or 'politeness' and relates to issues such as:

social behaviour: e.g. sharing, turn taking, respecting each other;

appropriate play: e.g. not throwing sand, wearing an apron to paint;

spoken language: e.g. speaking quietly and politely, not swearing, engaging in dialogue with others.

These conventions are guided by the moral values that you hold. They are concerned with creating a safe, respectful learning environment for adults and children alike.

Setting the standard of social behaviour

The social behaviours that have an impact on children's learning include the following:

- taking turns;
- sharing;
- showing respect to others;
- looking after resources.

Chapter 2 investigated moral behaviour and moral codes of conduct, and set out some ways in which you can demonstrate and encourage these values in your setting. If children are to be in a position to learn then you must expect these standards of behaviour at all times; you should encourage them, notice them when the children show them and praise and reward them. And this must be consistently applied by all members of staff. Part of your role is to make sure that every child has equal access to the learning that you offer them and these behaviours are necessary if you are to achieve this goal.

You must:

- expect;
- notice;
- reward.

Earlier chapters have looked at social conventions from the child's point of view, suggesting ways to help the children show this sort of behaviour. Let's now look in more detail at these four aspects of social behaviour from the adult's perspective, thinking of how you can model them.

> **TOP TIP!**
>
> *Imitation is the most effective route to improving the children's social behaviour for learning. You are the model for the children to copy, and they will be copying you whatever you are doing and whether you are anticipating it or not.*

Taking turns

If you work as part of a team you will have many opportunities to demonstrate taking turns. Children will soon recognise that today Sue is preparing the snacks and washing up, while Jan is helping children in the bathroom. They soon realise that you all share the different tasks out and do different things on different days. This is an easy way to show equality, that everyone sometimes has to do their least favourite job, that someone has to do the more unpleasant or boring jobs, because this is part of life. If the staff don't do this with a good grace then they can't expect the children to behave in any other way when they are asked to take turns in an activity or at clearing away.

Sharing

Sharing resources can cause friction between children when they are not prepared to let someone else play with them or alongside them. Children can be selfish at times, wanting all of the dough, or all of the bricks so that they can make a really big model. Does this ever happen amongst the staff? Are there times when someone uses up all of the expensive foil paper – and just for mounting some work – and you were planning to use it to make some festive decorations with the children? Resources are there for everyone to share, and this is a value that you should be demonstrating to the children, so that they can learn to curb their own plans if these will result in being unfair to others. If you want to use some resource that is in short supply or expensive – ask the manager's opinion. You may find that she is quite willing for you to use up the last of something, or the material that's been in the cupboard for ages. When you do your planning, check availability of the necessary resources at the same time and make sure that everyone gets a fair share of equipment, space and resources.

Sharing ideas is a superb way for the whole team to develop professionally. Newly qualified staff have the benefit of the latest training, and should have lots of up-to-date ideas that can benefit the whole staff. If this is you, then don't feel afraid to speak up. The staff members who have been trained for some time will have the benefit of experience to share. Be ready to listen to this and take advantage of their greater experience. If all the staff members can learn to work together, to tolerate each other and be prepared to learn from each other, the whole team will be more effective and, ultimately, the children will be the winners.

Why not try this?

Sharing ideas

- If you have been on a course, tell people about some of the interesting ideas that you heard. This might be a planned part of the next team meeting.

- If something worked well, tell others about it. Have a staff notebook that everyone can write in, where you can all record successful ideas for future reference.

- Have a card index file subdivided into curriculum areas. Write your activity idea on a card and file it away in the box, ready for the next planning session. This might detail an approach that you used for an activity, or an extension to an activity that you created in response to the children's interest in something.

- Have a concertina file subdivided into curriculum areas plus 'behaviour'. If you read a useful article in one of the professional magazines or journals cut it out and file it.

Respecting other people

Respect between fellow professionals is vital if you are to work as a team to benefit the children. When one member of staff is reading, trying to hold the attention of a group of children, it is most unhelpful for others to be chatting, or clearing away very close to them. When one adult is talking with a group of children round the table, it is distracting to the children if another adult voice is too loud, too near. Of course you have all got to get on with your work, but take time to think about such issues when you lay out the room, and when you plan your time with the children. Be aware of the volume of your own voice and moderate it to suit the circumstances. If you accidentally make a noise when the children are quietly listening, then apologise.

The behaviour you show, the way that you respect others, feeds into the children's growing repertoire of suitable behaviour, so always aim to set the highest standard you can achieve.

Looking after resources

If children are to look after resources you have to show them what you expect them to do and help them to do it. Resources should be kept in an organised way, grouped by use. Your room will reflect the six areas of the Early Years Foundation Stage or the Key Stage 1 curriculum, so the resources that children can access should be grouped in the same way and in the same area of your room. This means that, for example, all the number jigsaws and shape puzzles will be with the mathematical equipment, whereas all the life cycle puzzles will be with the material for Knowledge and Understanding of the World. Explain to the children how and why you have done this. Check after every session to make sure that resources are where they are meant to be. If you keep on top of the tidying up of resources you will always be able to find what you want.

> ### TOP TIP!
>
> *Children should not be expected to play with broken toys, do puzzles where pieces are missing or write and draw with blunt or minuscule crayons or dried-up felt pens. This is the responsibility of all the adults who work in the setting. At the end of each session check resources, replenish the cut paper and sharpen the pencils, repair anything where this can be done or throw it out if it can't be fixed. Don't hoard – 'in case of'! It's like the jumper with the curry stain on it – you won't wear it again no matter how much you paid for it or how beautiful it once was. The only thing to do is get rid of it and look after the next one more carefully. You can't expect children to show care and respect for rubbish. You have to set the example of care.*

Rules about appropriate play

Chapter 1 considered whether the children were aware of the rules that you keep in your setting, and ways to help them to remember those rules. At that point the main focus was on rules that kept the children safe, and routines that helped to keep things running smoothly. It is worth taking this a step further by now pinpointing the rules that help them to learn.

This would be a suitable Circle Time activity as part of your PSE curriculum.

Behaviour and Self-control: Development matters: 40–60+ months

Have an awareness of the boundaries set, and of behavioural expectations in the setting.

Take one activity that is available daily for the children and sit a group of children around it. Let's take the water-tray as an example.

Find out if the children know what rules you have.

How do they know them?

Are they written down? Can they read them?

Did someone tell them about the rules?

It's quite common for children to express rules in negative terms. It's worth noticing this and thinking – is it a reflection of how often staff say 'don't' or 'mustn't' to the children, and how infrequently they remind them of what it is they should be doing? Spend some time rephrasing any negative statements into positive ones. Work together on this so that the children start to see the connection between what they haven't got to do and what they should be doing instead. If appropriate, point out that these are opposites of each other.

Behaviour and Self-control: Effective practice: 40–60+ months

Ensure that children have opportunities to identify and discuss boundaries, so that they understand why they are there and what they are intended to achieve.

Now collect up all the rules for playing at the water-tray:

- Play carefully.
- Wear an apron.
- When indoors: mop up any spills or ask an adult to help you if there is a lot of water.

- Keep the toys in the container next to the water.
- Hang your apron up when you have finished.

TOP TIP!

Cut out some tiny 'aprons' from plastic carrier bags – choose bright colours. Draw a figure with a smiley face on a piece of card and stick one of the 'aprons' on it. Draw some 'hooks' on the piece of card and stick the other 'aprons' on as if they are hanging up. Use this as a label near water, paint or any other activity that needs aprons.

The children can help you to make labels like this. It may help them to remember the rule. (See www.pearsoned.co.uk/essentialguides for further ideas on this tip.)

You can repeat this process with any new piece of equipment that you are introducing to the children or as a reminder of ways to behave if you are experiencing some pattern of misuse of a particular resource. Children don't always know how to use a resource safely and may be simply copying other children's behaviour, so make sure that you correct inappropriate behaviour as soon as you spot it.

Once you have agreed on a set of rules your next step is to find ways to make the rules manageable for you and for the children.

Why not try this?

Keeping to the rules

Concentrate on just one of the rules in your setting.

- Write it at the top of a large sheet of paper.
- What does it mean? Brainstorm the practical application of this rule.
- What will we see happening when the rule is kept?
- How do the adults help the children?
- What resources do we offer the children to help them keep to this rule?
- Could we do more?

Here is an example of this activity in practice, as applied to taking turns to use the painting easels.

What do we mean?

- Children have to wait for their turn, letting others have a chance to enjoy the resource.

➜

- Children have to be prepared to stop their own involvement to let others have a turn.
- This is about fairness and equality of access to the resources in the setting.

What do we see?

- Only a set number of children use the easels at one time.
- Children have to watch out for their chance.
- Some children call to their friend when they are ready to go and their friend wants their place.
- Some children stay for a very long time, preventing others from having their turn.
- Some children get upset because they want to use it 'now' and are not very good at waiting.

What do we do to help?

- One person keeps an eye on the activity and makes sure that no one has a long turn if there are others waiting.
- We intervene to help the children understand that they will get a turn, but not at this minute.
- We remind those at the activity that others would also like a turn and their time will be limited.
- We make sure that if a child is concentrating and nearly finished then we allow them to complete their task.

Resources

- We make sure that there are sufficient resources available for all the children to be occupied with drawing/colouring/other art activities – across the setting. This means that everyone has a fair choice of art activity.
- We have a large supply of paper ready so that we don't waste time looking for paper if a child is waiting.

Could we do more?

- Remove wet paintings as quickly as possible to make space available.
- Have an additional easel outside on dry days.

Setting the standards of speech and conversation

As well as monitoring and supporting the children's ever-widening vocabulary and the degree of accuracy of their grammar, you should also be thinking about the way that speech indicates one person's awareness of the needs of others.

Speech can indicate the level of respect that a person is willing to give another person. This is connected with politeness. Saying 'please' and 'thank you', referring to someone by the right name, saying 'excuse me' or 'sorry' – these all show that you notice other people and what they are doing for you. It is always appreciated. As well as demonstrating this as adults – to other adults and to the children – you should be expecting this from the children. When they forget you should be reminding them, 'What do you say?' or 'Thank you ... who?' You should also notice when they do speak politely or respectfully and praise them for doing it.

> *Behaviour and Self-control: Look, listen and note: 40–60+ months*
>
> Children's increasing understanding of acceptable behaviour for themselves and others.

Holding a conversation needs input from at least two people. The very young baby interacts with the mother or other care-giver in an alternating pattern. The mother speaks and smiles at the baby, the baby gurgles and smiles at the mother, the mother smiles and speaks or makes a noise, the baby gurgles ... they are taking it in turns and having a 'conversation'.

> **TOP TIP!**
>
> *Eye contact is important whenever we enter into dialogue with another person. The convention in this country is that the person speaking looks briefly at the other person and then looks away. The person who is listening keeps their eyes focused on the speaker. This eye contact is a great help when you want a child to pay attention to what you are saying. 'Look at me' may often have to be the reminder that you give. It helps the child focus in on you, your face and your language.*

When two people are in conversation they should be taking it in turns to speak. One person should be listening to the other person. They should be following on the subject matter or picking up from something that the other person said. This demands good listening skills, eye contact and a willingness to take your turn.

Why not try this?

What about swearing?

This is a subject for debate amongst the whole staff. You should be considering issues such as:

- What constitutes swearing?
  - Are there any words that would offend specific children in this setting because of their racial or religious overtones?
  - Are there words that we use as adults that we don't want the children to use?
  - What do we think about the use of the street language that is used by many young people?
  - The last word on this will be for the manager, and it is then up to all members of staff to abide by her decision.
- How will we respond to swearing?
  - Create a list of phrases or responses that you could use. Try: 'That's not a word we use here', 'Can you think of a different word for that? ... That's a much better word to use.'

Remember to link your comment to what is acceptable in the setting. Parents may accept this language at home and you should avoid openly criticising the children's parents or undermining the children's respect for their parents.

Sometimes swearing is done for effect. On these occasions it is better ignored. To counteract it, be ready with lots of praise when the child says something without swearing, or uses a more appropriate word.

Developing a professional Code of Conduct within the setting

It is important that all members of staff play their part in the daily duties that are necessary for the setting to run efficiently and effectively, delivering a high-quality learning environment for the children. Established staff will know what is involved in each duty in this setting. A new member of staff or a trainee may not realise everything that is expected of them. This could lead to a situation where some job is not done, some area is left unsupervised or someone thinks another person isn't pulling their weight. It is, therefore, a good idea to make yourself aware of all that is entailed in any duty. For example:

When you are responsible for the bathroom, find out if it is also your responsibility to check the stock of nappies, or to mop up spills whenever the children wash their hands with great vigour!

When you are responsible for the outdoor area, are you expected just to set it up and supervise the clearing away, or do you have to be out there at all times during the session?

Why not try this?

What is involved in this area?

Spend a few minutes as a whole staff focusing on each area of the setting, making a list of the specific duties, e.g. outdoor, bathroom, snacks, lunches, house play, art, care of the animals. Each of these will have some duties that have to be carried out in every session, others will be done less often, perhaps just once a week. Identify the timescale as well as the tasks. There will also be some general duties regarding setting out or clearing away. Make lists for each of these. Include the minimum requirements and if you have time to spare you should be willing to do that extra task that will help things run smoothly.

Formats and ideas for these are on the website: www.pearsoned.co.uk/essentialguides.

Keep these lists in the staff handbook and make sure that everyone knows about them. If you have a student in, and she is working in a specific area during one session, ask her to read through the appropriate list so that she knows what she should and shouldn't be doing.

The developing brain: discovering your world

You receive information about the world through your sense organs – your eyes, ears, nose, tongue and skin. This information takes the form of light waves, sound waves or molecular structure (providing you with a sense of the feel of things, whether they are hard, fluffy, cold, etc.). The sense organs turn these stimuli into electrical pulses. These pulses follow neural paths (neurons are cells that are designed to pass on electrical impulses) towards specific areas of the brain. Along the way the pulses may be split, with some going to the cerebral cortex and others to the limbic system.

In the cerebral cortex (the outer layer of the brain) the different pulses can be linked with each other so that you recognise things.

Imagine you are presented with a cup; your eyes only see brown liquid but your nose smells the aroma of coffee and your hand feels the heat. You need all of this information to register that what you have is indeed a cup of coffee, and your sense of taste will confirm this.

The pulses that go to the limbic system generate emotional responses, such as a sense of beauty when you look at a particular view or the panic you feel when you hear the fire alarm going off.

Each area of the cerebral cortex that is devoted to a specific sense has its own subdivisions. For example, the visual cortex separates incoming stimuli into motion, colour, shape, brightness, etc. Different people construct the world in slightly different ways according to the number of cells they have in any one of these subdivisions.

In the very young baby any stimulus can be represented in any way as the neural paths that divide up the incoming stimuli are not firmly set. Some people continue to experience the world like this and may describe Tuesday as 'yellow', for example. It is only as the cortex develops that the brain starts to categorise the stimuli. This process is useful as it speeds up your identification of the stimuli.

Behaviour that is part of the learning process

Before beginning to think about the learning behaviour that you are hoping to see it is worth taking some time to examine more closely exactly what is meant by 'learning'. There are other publications that deal with learning styles or schema – the way that individual children learn. The concern here is with the physical and mental processes that are necessary for learning to take place and the behaviours that allow this to happen in constructive and positive ways.

The skills of learning

The learning process starts when the children take notice of their surroundings and the many stimuli around them. They then have to respond in some way, to process that information or gather more evidence or clarification. This new learning is then added to their store of knowledge or used in other circumstances to make sense of the next step of learning.

TOP TIP!

To learn children have to:

● take notice of the stimuli around them;

● respond to the stimuli;

● apply the learning.

The various processes which could be involved in each of these steps are summarised in the table below. Whenever you are planning the children's learning try taking these processes into account and finding ways to incorporate them as learning tools. Whenever your children are engaged in learning you should be able to notice which processes they are using. It is worth identifying opportunities to focus on these different processes, and note these in your planning so that you don't miss a chance to develop the children's behaviour for learning.

The learning process		
Notice the stimuli around you	**Respond**	**Apply the learning**
• look • listen • feel • smell • taste	• think about the stimulus • interpret the stimulus • investigate its nature and potential • question self, others and resources for additional information • remember new information, organising and categorising it	• think through potential actions • engage in inner speech • consider the options • apply existing and new information and skills to new situations • communicate your learning to others

As you think about these three steps consider:

● what it means for you as a provider of education, play and learning;

● what it means for the children as learners;

● how you can influence these steps to learning in practical ways each day.

Taking notice

The children live in an environment full of sights and sounds, some new and some familiar. There are tastes, textures and smells all around. Learning starts when the children take notice of these stimuli. It is your role to draw the children's attention to the stimuli that are around them in all their different forms.

Responding

As the children absorb the information from the stimuli they will be responding in different ways. The particular response they make may reflect the nature of the stimulus, the guidance of the adult or the preferred way of the individual child.

Reflecting on practice

Jay, 5.7 years and Luke, 5.8 years

Jay and Luke were good friends who usually played together. They had been looking at a new picture book about sea creatures. Each page had a beautiful illustration and some facts about the creature.

Jay later drew an outline of a whale. It was on the largest piece of paper he could find. He filled in the outline with a twisting, curling, squiggly line, and then filled in all the spaces with different colours. He added strips of tissue seaweed, and surrounded the whale with smaller fish in bright colours.

Luke was fascinated by the facts. He made a list of the creatures in size order. He wanted to know about the sizes of other whales. Was this the biggest? What was the smallest size of whale?

Consider the following:

1. When you observe the children's responses to the stimuli you provide for them be aware of all the ways in which they may have been influenced.

2. In this case, from the same stimulus, both boys were inspired in different ways; one by the illustrations, one by the factual information. Or were they both interested in size? Look again at what Jay did – he needed the largest sheet of paper he could find. He drew the whale much larger than the other fish. The colouring-in was stylised, not factual, but maybe that was because he couldn't concentrate long enough to colour in such a large space with just one crayon.

The child will first have to think about the stimulus. In child-led activities these will be the child's own thoughts. In adult-led activities you may be questioning the child. What sort of questions will you ask? It is worth including some ideas in your planning notes. Do they allow the child to 'ponder', to think around the question? Questions to which the child can answer 'yes' or 'no' or give direct obvious replies offer no challenge and very little space for quality thinking or personal development.

From this initial thinking will come choices about optional ways to respond. The child might be encouraged to explore and investigate the stimulus further. What will happen if we add water? What will we get if we mix these together? The child might have more questions he wants answered and need resources available – including adults for younger children but books for those who can read – as he seeks more information or clarification. Above all, he needs time and space.

Dispositions and Attitudes: Effective practice: 30–50 months

Encourage children to see adults as a resource and as partners in their learning.

Applying their learning

The children need to manipulate what they have experienced and found out in order to truly learn something. It is said that real learning is shown when someone, child or adult, can take something that they have learnt in one context and use it in another set of circumstances. Compare the pages of 'sums' that you did in school with the way you have to work out your budget or find out whether the wonderful loan you've been offered is such a bargain after all.

TOP TIP!

To reflect on what they have observed children need the guidance of adults. They need help to see how this piece of information fits in with all the other pieces of information the child already has. Learning is about making connections. It is the responsibility of the adult to point these out to the child. Take time to remind them of earlier learning.

When you have drawn attention to a new stimulus and asked relevant questions that led the child to find out more, your next step is to challenge their perceptions and their thinking as a positive way to develop their ideas. Cathy Nutbrown (2006, p 5) urges practitioners to encourage children to 'articulate their thinking' as this helps you to help them 'refine and further develop their ideas'. Reflective thinking, when voiced by the child, should be supported. Give time for them to explain as best they can. Help them to refine their vocabulary if they get stuck – making sure that you have allowed them enough time to self-correct. Ask interested and challenging questions. But above all, respect their efforts. Don't laugh at mistakes or misguided ideas. Don't use sarcasm to put down their thoughts.

> ### Dispositions and Attitudes: Effective practice: 40–60+ months
>
> Encourage children to explore and talk about what they are learning, valuing their ideas and ways of doing things.

Talking about learning behaviour

Think of words such as 'explore', 'investigate', 'find out about', 'ask questions', 'show curiosity', 'be interested', 'focus on', 'recreate', 'use language', 'use numbers'. All of these expressions are taken from the Development Matters section of the EYFS. These expressions are the guides for the learning behaviour that you are encouraging the children to develop. Don't ignore them in your records or your planning.

> ### TOP TIP!
>
> When you write out the learning objectives for your planned activities make reference to the learning behaviours as well as to any specific knowledge or skill that you will be focused on.
>
> Wednesday, 5 May
>
> EYFS area: Knowledge and understanding of the world
>
> EYFS aspect: Exploration and investigation
>
> Learning objective: ELG: Find out about, and identify, some features of living things ... they observe
>
> Learning behaviour: At the pond: Observe, investigate, be curious
> Back in the room: Use books, ask questions, look at posters
>
> Activities: Take nets and jars to the pond, ... etc.
>
> Resources: Nets, jars, books, ... etc.
>
> Learning outcomes: Models/painting/ ... etc.

Remind the children of what they are doing as the activity proceeds. Tell them quite explicitly.

'We are going to look at the pond today.'

'We will be looking for …'

'We might see …'

'We can observe … closely with our magnifiers.'

'When we get back to the room we will be finding out more.'

'We will be exploring out here.'

'We will be investigating the pond to find out what lives in it.'

Give them the language of learning and respond with praise when they use it.

If your children know how to learn they can go from strength to strength. They can use the opportunities that you and later teachers will provide. They can learn from every aspect of their daily life. You will be giving them a wonderful start in life.

Learning behaviour

The level of success that the children achieve is partly due to the quality of their actions as they engage in the learning processes described in the table on page 153. So in this context the term 'behaviour' describes the quality of the children's actions.

Are you looking?

There's a painting hanging in your hall, you look at it every day as you put your bag down when you get home. You don't actually stop to look at it, it's just there, although you'd probably notice if it disappeared one day.

You visit an art gallery and stand in front of each picture in turn, noticing the shape, form or colour and thinking about the artist's intentions.

The difference between these two experiences of 'looking' is that you paid attention to the art gallery pictures, you took time to concentrate on them and think about them. On the other hand you merely glanced at the picture in your hall.

So, this exploration of the process of learning suggests that the specific behaviours the children need to develop in order to learn are:

- paying attention;
- concentrating.

Paying attention

You want the children to pay attention to the specific stimuli which you have planned or identified, to look around them in such a way that they notice what is there. This might be a natural event (a snowstorm, fog, spring flowers, autumn colour), part of their physical environment (buildings and people they pass, the farm, the new houses going up next to your setting) or the stimuli you choose to set out for them (the ice cubes and polar bears you put in the water-tray, the display of red objects you set out on the cupboard top, the new books in the book box).

Young children have a short attention span because the part of the brain responsible for this is not fully mature. The new-born's brain has still to create a coating of myelin around the individual parts of the brain. This is a gradual process. Until the myelin is in place that part of the brain can't receive electrical impulses. This sheathing of myelin doesn't occur in the part of the frontal lobes that is responsible for attention until the child reaches or even completes puberty.

Dispositions and Attitudes: Effective practice: 22–36 months

Recognise that children's interest may last for short or long periods, and that their interests and preferences vary.

Things you can do to help you get the children's attention:

- To compensate for the child's short attention span be prepared to change activity frequently, so that the child focuses on the new thing, or the next stage or development of the original stimulus. Don't abandon the original stimulus, but be ready to have a break from it and come back to it later, or shift your focus to another aspect of the same stimulus.

- The stimulus will exist whether the child looks at it or not. Take a moment to look around your setting and see which table-top displays are being handled by children, whether there are any areas that are devoid of children, and whether you notice any child looking at a wall display?

- Displays soon lose their impact and become no more use than wallpaper. It doesn't matter how long it took you to put it up, or how proud of it you are – if the children have stopped paying attention to it then it has no more use. Sometimes you might be able to modify your display. Put up some paintings one week. Next week do some writing about them and then add that to the display.

- Are your displays visible to the children? Get down on your knees and look at the room from the child's perspective. Alter them if you need to, so that the children can see details on your wall display or touch objects on the table top. In other words – give them a fighting chance of paying attention!

- As Brierley states (1994, p 111): 'The brain thrives on variety and stimulation. Monotony of surroundings, toys that only do one thing, a classroom display kept up for too long are soon disregarded by the brain.' Notice that he writes 'by the brain' not 'by the child'. It is a natural response. You have to work with this knowledge, not against it.

- Activities that need adult input, where you expect the children to listen and concentrate on your words, or enter into a discussion, need to be positioned away from more physical activities such as water or paint.

- Plan time for the children to tell you about things they have seen when out with their parents, or on the way in that morning. Give time and encouragement. Ask questions and show that you are interested in their observations. Include other children in the discussion.

- Ask the children: 'What is different in the setting this morning?' If necessary give them clues – 'It's on the wall', 'It's outside'.

- Play a 'trick'. For example, remove all of the 't' letters in the display notices, or cover them over. Then introduce them to that letter as part of their language/phonic work.

- If there's an odd moment when you are waiting for all the children to gather together ask them: 'Who can spot five books?', 'Who can name something green in our room?', 'Point to something yellow', 'Point to a picture of a zebra' and so on.

Concentration

If you want children to do more than just gaze upon their environment you have to be committed to engaging them in investigation and exploration. You have to observe them and encourage them when they interact with their surroundings. You have to allow them time to assimilate as much as they can, in any way that works for them. You have to be ready to aid their discoveries and supply additional resources or information.

Things you can do to help your children concentrate:

- Remembering the child's short attention span, make sure that you plan activities in small chunks so that they can be completed in a short time. Those children who can concentrate for longer can take the activity further, so have some ideas planned for additional activities that will extend the learning.

Dispositions and Attitudes: Development matters: 40–60+ months

Persist for extended periods of time at an activity of their choosing.

- If a child can complete a task he will feel a sense of personal achievement. This promotes high self-esteem. The child will view himself as an accomplished learner and be ready to tackle the next challenge with positive expectations.

Dispositions and Attitudes: Effective practice: 40–60+ months

Give children opportunities to complete activities to their satisfaction.

- Have a clearly defined end in sight. This should be the planned learning objective, not necessarily the finished result. For example:
  - You want the children to notice similarities and differences in shapes and sizes.
  - Everyone has a piece of dough of the same weight. Use the balance to prove this.
  - Everyone makes a model with their dough, making sure that they use it all; they might make animals, shapes, monsters or long snakes.
  - Balance the models when they are completed. They all weigh the same but they all look different.

  You haven't told them what to make, their end results are individual, you can value everyone's model, their ideas and skills of using their dough, but it is important that you also make time to praise the children for the fact that they concentrated and completed the task.

- Allowing time for the children to follow something through to its conclusion is possibly one of the hardest things for you to do when you are trying to juggle a full curriculum and still comply with all the rules and regulations, assessments and record keeping. But it is possible. Come back to the same activity – with a twist or a development. For example:

- Set out your new train track on Monday – just the track and some engines and carriages.

- On Tuesday add some houses and trees to make a village near the station.

- On Wednesday add the farm set to make some countryside for the train to go through.

- On Thursday lay out a large piece of paper to paint a backdrop for the train set. Try trees, flowers, houses or whatever your children are able to reproduce. When it is dry pin it up behind the train.

- On Friday make up some travel stories: 'Gran got on the train at … She went to … On the way she saw …'

● Do some activities over a number of days. For example:

- On Friday, lay out a large piece of plastic such as an opened-out black sack. Children use PVA glue to stick torn pieces of tissue on it – laid flat, and overlapping in places. Leave it to dry over the weekend.

- On Monday, peel the tissue away from the plastic backing, cut it out into a butterfly shape and attach it to one of your windows to let the light shine through.

The gap in time encourages the children to remember. Include a Learning Objective in your planning notes to show that you have deliberately chosen to run an activity over several days to encourage sustained concentration.

● When children are allowed to extend their own activities over more than one session they are being given a chance to remember. They can absorb today's learning and reconsider it tomorrow. They can change it or amend it in light of later thoughts or because they have realised that they can build something differently or more effectively. They can see that you recognise their efforts are important. It promotes quality rather than superficiality.

● Encourage children to go back to a piece of work. They can embellish or change it, add some paint, stick on some sparkly bits, make a label or cut out or mount their drawing. At the same time you must be prepared to acknowledge it when the child states that he has completed a piece of work.

Reflecting on practice

Becky, aged 3.4 years

A large sheet of paper was on the easel. Becky asked for her name to be put on it. She donned her apron, took some time to choose a brush and then looked with concentration at the available colours. She loaded the brush eventually with lots of brown paint. She then carefully put the brush →

to the paper, drawing it down for about five centimetres, replaced the brush in the pot and removed her apron before going off to wash her hands.

As her key worker said, 'The true artist knows when to stop!'

Consider the following:

1. The care taken showed that Becky saw this as a complete piece of work. Would you have encouraged Becky to do more?
2. How might the key worker have taken this further?
3. Would you have engaged Becky in discussion of her work when she had returned from washing her hands?

In touch with parents – helping your child to learn

The level of parents' involvement in their child's learning varies enormously. At one extreme there will be the parents who ignore their child, spending their time doing what they want to do, and dragging the child along behind them. And at the other end of the scale are the parents who are continually pushing their child, comparing his achievements to those of the others in his class, or his brother, or something they read in a magazine.

How can you help the parents to find a balance? One way is to prepare some lists that could be included in your regular newsletter to parents, or produced as individual leaflets which they can pick up or you can hand out at appropriate times. If you do prepare something in response to one parent's request, make it available to others. Keep a stockpile of your ideas.

Why not try this?

Helping your child to learn at home

Behaviour is the focus of these specific ideas, but you could extend the idea and make lists for different aspects of the rest of the EYFS.

Decide on your focus and write it at the top of a piece of A4 paper. Pin it on the staff notice board for a week and encourage anyone else to add their ideas. When you have a good supply go through them, check their suitability and then transfer the information to your computer and produce a leaflet. Put your setting's name and any logo at the top, and contact details at the bottom.

→

Here are a few suggestions to start with (see www.pearsoned.co.uk/essential guides for more ideas):

Learning to share

Buy sweets that have to be shared, e.g. a bar of chocolate between you, rather than always giving the child his own packet or bar.

Buy a toy that needs to be shared in order to be played, such as a cricket set of bat and ball, or a board game or pack of cards.

Be prepared to share your things and your time: play the game with him, give him some chocolates from the box that you were given.

Join the library so that your child can borrow a book that isn't his. Looking after someone else's property and then understanding that he needs to give it back means that other children will be more prepared to share their things with your child.

Learning to take turns

If you have more than one child at home try to let one child choose one day, and the other on the next day: who has which seat in the car, which book you will read to them at bedtime, the route you take to school.

Play board games that involve taking turns to move your piece or throw the dice.

Looking after your property

Provide boxes for toys and make sure that they are used every night before bedtime.

Help your child to put dirty clothes in the laundry basket or shoes in the cupboard, and insist on it every day.

Help your child to tidy away – the dishes, the toys, the clothes – look for any opportunity that you can think of. Make a fun time out of it. Sing 'This is the way we pick up the bricks', etc. (to the tune of 'Here we go round the mulberry bush'). Or set the timer and have a race. Can we beat the timer?

Learning to look after yourself

Encourage independent dressing. Lay clothes out in the right order, with underwear at the top and jumpers at the bottom of the pile.

Point out labels on clothes and where they usually go – jumper labels at the back, for example.

Choose clothes with easy fastenings at this stage – zips and Velcro® or pull-ons.

Practise flushing the toilet and washing hands after every visit.

→

Learn about yourself

Know their full name.

Know their telephone number.

Know their birthday.

Know their address.

Explain to parents the importance of having this information – just in case they ever get lost. It's a life skill that they should have. It will help them to keep safe.

Conclusion

This chapter has examined how children can behave in ways that allow them to learn, and allow others around them to learn.

This happens when you create the sort of atmosphere that will encourage and support learning. This includes the children helping to look after the resources and equipment that you provide for them. They also should be speaking with others in ways that demonstrate their respect for the other person, being polite, using appropriate language and taking part in conversations.

If children are to engage in learning they also need to be helped to learn how to learn. They need to know about listening, exploring, thinking, investigating – all the processes that are needed if learning is to take place. These are lifelong skills and will benefit the children for the whole of their future.

Key ideas summary

You now have an understanding that if your children are to learn you have to take a dual approach:

You have to create the right atmosphere, where:

● staff set a standard of social behaviour for children to model by being willing to take turns and share the workload;

● staff look after the resources and encourage the children to do the same;

● everyone speaks to each other with respect and consideration;

→

You have to plan ways to promote the behaviour that is necessary for learning:

- by understanding the processes involved in learning – notice, respond, react;
- by understanding the way that the brain's development affects children's ability to notice and concentrate;
- by helping children to pay attention;
- by thinking of ideas to encourage concentration.

Going further

A useful starting point for finding out more about how children learn is *The Brain's Behind It* by Alistair Smith. This provides information on how the brain functions and how that affects learning.

Smith, A. (2002) *The Brain's Behind It*, Stafford: Network Educational Press.

Squirrel says

On Sunday, Squirrel had made a decision. He was going to buy a computer so that he could write a book. He didn't know which one would be best for him so he went to number 7, and rang the bell. Mr Ferret used his computer a lot, so Squirrel thought he would be a good person to ask.

On Monday, Squirrel went to the big shop that sold lots of different computers. He knew the sort of computer he wanted, Mr Ferret had helped him to decide – but there were so many others to choose from. He went to the saleslady and asked her opinion.

On Tuesday, Squirrel had managed to set up his computer – Mr Ferret had come over and helped him when he got stuck. Now he had to read the book to find out how to start using his computer.

On Wednesday, Squirrel still hadn't managed to start using his computer. It was half-past three and he had made himself a cup of tea – perhaps that would help him to think more clearly and sort out all the information. The children were coming home from school.

→

'That's it!' said Squirrel. He left his cup of tea on the side and rushed off down the stairs. 'Children!' he called. 'Children! You know about computers. Don't you?'

'Of course we do,' said the children.

'I would be ever so grateful if any of you could come and help me with mine,' said Squirrel.

'I'll help you,' said Vernon Vole.

'So will I', said Fergie Ferret.

'Well, go home first and ask your parents if that's all right,' said Squirrel.

On Thursday Squirrel started to write his book.

Squirrel says,

'If you want to find things out you have to be willing to ask other people to help you when you get stuck.'

Develop a positive outlook on life

What this chapter will explore:

- The growth of self-assurance
- How children learn to solve problems
- How to help children face stressful situations
- How to encourage children to engage with learning in a positive way

This chapter will focus on how a child can be helped to develop a positive outlook on life so that he will feel confident to deal with whatever turns up in his life.

A child who has high self-esteem and emotional strength will have *inner* self-confidence, for these are internal states. The next step in developing his behaviour is to take him to a point where he is *outwardly* confident of his own abilities. This will be the factor that allows him to anticipate new challenges with excitement and pleasure, even if he is a little apprehensive.

Self-assurance

Chapter 6 dealt with the child's growing sense of self as a precursor to developing self-esteem. This also plays a part in building the child's confidence in his own abilities to cope with life. This self-awareness can be seen in the young child as he learns more about himself, and as he learns about other people.

By two years of age the child knows that he is a separate person, that he has a 'self'. With this awareness of self comes the awareness that sometimes he has done something wrong and that sometimes he has done the right thing; he knows about right and wrong. He recognises when things have been damaged, and he can feel guilty if he thinks, or knows, that he has caused it. He seeks the approval of adults and notices the signs of approval and disapproval. He can feel pride in his own achievements. He knows the standards of behaviour in the home and starts to use these as a guide to check his own behaviour. When he has been in the setting for some time he will start to do the same with the standards he sees there.

His knowledge and awareness of other people is also developing. At two he knows that others have feelings. By the age of four he knows that these feelings may be different from his own feelings. He recognises that his actions may hurt others; he knows about consequences and he can decide to moderate his behaviour. By the time he is three he begins to understand that other people have intentions; if they are about to do something and get distracted, then he can recognise and finish their task.

All of this knowledge allows the child to grow into a self-assured person. He understands himself. He understands what makes others tick.

He is now ready to work comfortably within the wider social context and to deal with the different events that will happen in his life. He will be ready to deal with:

● the challenges of living;
● the challenges of learning.

You can actively help him to acquire the skills he needs to sort out problems, so that he can enjoy and embrace the challenge of learning. At the same time you have to remain vigilant for any extreme circumstances that might occur in his life.

TOP TIP!

Your responses and your behaviour towards a child will be influential on how he copes now, and on the sort of attitude towards problems or stress that he will take with him into adult life.

Problem solving

Problem solving means that you think through a problem.

Why not try this?

What is 'thinking'?

Working with a few colleagues, brainstorm your ideas about 'thinking'.

Using your ideas, try to create a definition that you can all agree with. Here are a few suggestions to start your discussion:

- Thinking involves recollecting and imagining.
- Thinking demands a degree of self-awareness.
- Thinking means that you are 'holding ideas in mind and manipulating them' (Carter, 2003, p 312).
- When you think you focus your mind.
- Thinking means that you are paying attention to the subject matter and ignoring irrelevant stimuli.
- Thinking helps you to make the most of the opportunities to learn.
- Thinking is an active process.

When you stop and think you become more aware of all the possibilities, and then you consider these possibilities. You think about the choices you can make, of what you can do or what you might avoid doing.

Your role is to help the children to see 'problems' as challenges, and to know that they can take on the challenge and overcome or deal with it. It helps them to deal with life and life events – and not just to react with immoderate or antisocial behaviour when things don't go their way.

There will be times when the children have to face a dilemma and need the skills to think about the situation, their options, the potential consequences – and then make a choice. Some of these issues could even be life threatening.

Children from about four years old could be given problem-solving activities as part of their PSE work. It is important that as part of their personal behaviour management they learn how to face tricky situations.

> ### Dispositions and Attitudes: Planning and resourcing: 40–60+ months
>
> Provide experiences and activities that are challenging but achievable.

Learning to solve problems in the controlled setting of the classroom is one approach. You can take 'problems' and set them into familiar contexts for children to think about how they would sort things out, or how they would respond. You can do this for all aspects of the curriculum although the ideas given here focus on behaviour-related problems.

The skills that children need to develop if they are to have success with this are:

- the social skills that enable them to work with others and relate to others;
- the language and communication skills to talk about the problem and its possible resolutions;
- the emotional stability to feel able to investigate and explore.

The child who is self-assured, self-confident and friendly is going to have more success with these skills than a shy, retiring, anxious child.

> ### Dispositions and Attitudes: Look, listen and note: 40–60+ months
>
> Reactions to new activities and experiences, understanding that for some children such experiences can be both exciting and worrying.

Think about this when you group the children for these activities, so that there is always a mixture of characters.

Reflecting on practice

Richard, aged 7.8 years

Richard's case was an extreme one. He suffered from severe anxiety, so severe that he was in a special school.

Every time he came to the end of a line in his exercise book he panicked. 'There's no more space!' he would cry. He didn't know what to do. He had

→

to be coaxed to try the next line, which had lots of space on it. And this happened for every line. He gradually realised that he could do this himself – that he could go on to the next line without having a panic attack. Now his big problem was what to do when he reached the end of the page and there was no more space.

Richard needed a lot of patience and time to help him overcome this anxiety. The teacher worked on this while other specialists dealt with the underlying situation that had caused this problem for this little boy.

Consider the following:

1. Some children view a challenge or a problem as a source of great anxiety, as a mountain that they don't feel ready to climb. They may panic, withdraw or avoid.

   ● How will you help them?

2. Your role will be to encourage, and to help them to deal with only a tiny part of the challenge at a time. Then praise the child for his success. Show him that he is competent.

   ● How can you encourage them?

Set varying problems at different times to allow different children to take the lead. Some children will appear as the confident ones when the problem is based on, for example, a practical issue – 'How will you get this heavy box of bricks outside? It's far too heavy for anyone here to lift.' Others will be the confident ones when the problem is about making something – 'We need to create a shelter because it's too hot to sit outside today. Can you think how we can do this?' Try to give everyone a chance to display their strengths and so boost their self-esteem and their self-confidence, so that everyone can say, 'I can do this!'

Role play

Describe a scene. Discuss it as a whole group. Talk about the suggestions the children make and the consequences of each idea. Let the children work in threes or fours to practise their own idea – or the most suitable one. Gather together again, and talk about what it felt like to sort this problem out. Was there only one way to solve the problem? Was there a 'best' way to solve it?

Some ideas you can start with:

● Angie is at home. Her mummy falls down and can't get up. What should she do?

- Bennie has a cat. The cat is missing. How can Bennie try to find her?
- Charlie has a baby brother who is crawling and getting into everything. Charlie has a new set of building bricks. His little brother is always trying to get them but mummy says that he mustn't let the baby get the pieces because they are so small. What can Charlie do so that he can still play with the bricks?

These problems rely on the children having a well-developed sense of empathy as well as some practical skills.

Outdoor challenges – team work

> *Dispositions and Attitudes: Planning and resourcing: 30–50 months*
>
> Plan activities that require collaboration.

Don't get wet!

Make a paper or fabric 'puddle' that is wider than any equipment you have outdoors. Working in threes, the children have to find a way to get over the puddle without getting wet. Set this in a story, tell them how deep it is or about the crocodile that lives in it. Provide a few pieces of equipment. Everyone in the group has to be able to get across using the chosen method.

Will they work as a group?

Will one child take the lead, giving others a task, or will he take over and dominate?

How will the shy child react if he has a really good idea?

Save the bear!

Before the children arrive, place a teddy as high up as you can – in a tree or bush or on top of the railings. Explain the problem to the children and tell them that you need their help to rescue the bear. They have to work in threes to work out a rescue plan that you can carry out. They mustn't hurt teddy. If he falls he'll get hurt. The children tell you their plans and you all discuss each one and decide if it's worth trying. Don't try any of them out until everyone has told you their idea, just in case the first plan works!

Do the children recognise which actions might hurt teddy?

The challenges of living

Stressful situations may occur at any time for some of your children.

TOP TIP!

At times of stress children need to have their normal routine as a sign that the world and their life does carry on despite their unhappiness. Understand their mood swings but don't change your boundaries.

You won't necessarily know in advance when it will happen, so it is good practice to be prepared. Have some packs ready – information for parents, contact details for outside support, perhaps some books that you can share with the children or lend to parents to share with their children at home.

Why not try this?

In one school staff prepared some sets of information on death, bereavement, divorce, serious illness, etc. They consisted of zipped-top plastic bags, clearly labelled, and each containing a selection of leaflets for parents, information and guidance for teachers, some suggestions for activities, and a story book on the given 'situation'.

These were affectionately referred to as 'the dead rabbit packs' – everyone knew what it meant, and it took the sharpness off the words and the content. And it reminded staff that for a young child even this can be a devastating moment in their lives that needs sensitive handling.

A family member dies

The child's response will be individual to him, but will be affected by the facts of the particular situation. If a sibling dies both parents may be unavailable for the child and the child may not want to 'bother them'. If a parent dies the surviving parent may find it difficult to deal with their own grief and manage the household as well. The child may feel guilty that he caused the death because of his own behaviour towards the person. He may not understand the finality of death and be wondering when the person will come back.

Behaviours you may observe

- Regression.
- Lack of concentration.
- Anxiety when leaving the parent.
- Withdrawal.

Actions you can take

- Check with the family to find out what they have told their child and the general approach they would like you to follow.
- Within these boundaries answer any questions honestly and patiently, no matter how many times the child needs to ask them.
- Be prepared to let the child talk to you if he wants to.
- If the child wants to act out their concerns sit together at the 'small world' toys, such as a house or hospital, and be ready to listen.

'Grown-up human beings since the beginning of historical times have understood that the way to make contact with a child and to understand his way of thought is to play with him.'

(Urwin and Hood-Williams, 1988, p 266)

> ## TOP TIP!
>
> *To help children who are disturbed by events in their life, place some small world figures (people, buildings, vehicles, cute and scary animals, etc.) alongside your sand-tray, in a quiet area. As children play with small world figures in the sand watch what they are doing with them. Make comments about the actions of the figures – never the child.*
>
> *'I notice that you put the ... in the ...'*
>
> *Don't expect an answer.*
>
> *Don't make assumptions; describe only what you actually see.*
>
> *Don't try to interpret what you see.*
>
> *Your role is simply to express in words what the child is acting out with the figures.*
>
> *For more information about this see the work of Jenner (1999) and Lowenfeld (in Unwin and Hood-Williams, 1988).*

Parents split up

This can be preceded by conflict and upset. It may be accompanied by financial concerns, a change of home, anxiety about the missing parent or general disorganisation in the home.

Behaviours you may observe

- Anger and aggression.
- Younger children may be anxious and want to be near an adult all of the time.
- Before the actual separation occurs there may be conflict in the home that the child may act out in his play.
- Once the parent has left the home you may also see the sorts of behaviours associated with bereavement and loss.

Actions you can take

- Respect any information that the child discloses to you.
- Have the same expectations of his behaviour as before so that the child knows that some things don't change.
- Respond to his anger with a firm but kind manner, explaining that you understand how he feels, but that he mustn't hurt others by his words or actions.

> **TOP TIP!**
>
> When dealing with an angry child, provide a very physical activity to help him let off steam – kicking a ball at a goal, pummelling some dough, giving all the blankets a good shake outside in the fresh air.
>
> Let him draw his anger, then scrunch up the piece of paper and throw it away.
>
> Older children might be able to write a letter and then scrunch it up and throw it away or shred it so that the child feels safe, knowing that the person will never actually read the words that he wrote.

A parent is in prison

In many ways this can be like a death in the family. It can be accompanied by shame and guilt. Parents may hide the truth from their children. Children may be asked to keep secrets to prevent neighbours knowing what has happened. There may be changed circumstances – the remaining parent may need to work longer hours, there may be financial constraints, there may be some members of the family who have stopped visiting the home.

Behaviours you may observe

- Clinging to parent on arrival.
- Anxiety that the remaining parent is going to suddenly disappear.
- Withdrawal.
- Other children or parents may be abusive or may ignore the family.
- Visits to the prison may evoke anxiety, excitement or fear.

Actions you might take

- If you only hear about this through gossip, say nothing to the child. Be prepared for the time when the child may want to disclose information to you. Treat such information with absolute confidentiality.
- If it is public knowledge or the parent talks to you, find out what they have told the child and how they would like the situation to be handled.
- Before and after visits be prepared to allow the child an opportunity to talk quietly with you.
- You may need to respond as you would for a child who has been through a death or the divorce of his parents.

Transition

This occurs throughout life and includes starting at nursery, moving to a new class, a new teacher arriving, moving to the next school, moving house, etc. It is part of life and if you help a child to deal with change positively when he is young, helping him to see the excitement, the challenge and the possibilities it holds, he will be more able to deal with change in a positive way as an adult.

Behaviours you may observe

- Anxious and clinging to key worker.
- Poor sleep may leave the child short-tempered and easily upset or tearful.
- Reverting to immature behaviour.

Moving to the next stage of schooling

Why not try this?

Going to 'big school'

Imagine that you are the four year old about to leave nursery and go to school. Make a list of all the concerns you may have.

Once you have your list check it against the suggestions in the box on page 178.

Self-confidence and Self-esteem: Planning and resourcing: 40–60+ months

Plan Circle Times when children can have an opportunity to talk about their feelings and support them by providing props, such as a sad puppet, that can be used to show how they feel.

Actions to take when moving to the next stage of schooling:

- Talk about the move in PSE sessions and Circle Time.

- Read books about children going to school.

- Liaise with the schools that take your children and set up visits – you and the children to their new school, their new teacher to one of your sessions. This should be in addition to any visits the school arranges for parents and their children.

- The teacher at the school could take photographs of the children when they start, doing some 'school' activities – on the playground, in the hall, at assembly – activities that are new to the children. She could also take some other photographs of familiar activities – painting, sand, construction toys, reading and writing or drawing, etc. These could be made into a book with a caption for each picture, created by the children. This book can then be given to the nursery or pre-school to share with their children. The children will enjoy seeing their old friends at 'big school'.

- Arrange for some Year One children, who will know the new children, to escort them to lunch or outside at playtimes. Tell the children this will happen as you know that it can be tricky to remember where everything is and what they should be doing. Reassure them that they will soon remember all these things.

Possible concerns on starting at big school

- The building is huge and I might get lost.
- My mummy might forget where I am and not be able to find me in this huge place.
- It's very noisy.
- There are loads of people here.
- I don't know which is my room.
- How do I get to my room?
- Where are the toilets?
- Who do I ask if I want to go to the toilet?
- Where do I put my coat?
- Where do I leave my lunchbox?
- Will someone tell me when to have my lunch?
- Who will help me open my yogurt?
- Where will my mummy be when I want to find her?
- What is assembly?
- How do I put my shorts on?
- Where are my shorts?
- I can't remember what my new coat looks like.
- I can't fasten my own shoes – will anyone help me?
- I don't know how to read – will the teacher be cross?
- I've forgotten my teacher's name.

Moving to a new area or town

This can be stressful on many levels. Despite any excitement, parents will have practical concerns, possibly some financial worries, and everything will be in a muddle as the house is packed up. Children can find this very unsettling. Small children can make strange assumptions. Will my toys be left behind? Will there be any toys in the new house? Will we be taking the bath with us? Some children think it's like going on holiday and after a week or two in the new house they feel ready to move back 'home' again.

There are two situations you may have to face with your children:

1. When they are about to move house and maybe nursery as well, so leaving you and their friends behind.

2. When you receive new children who have just moved into your area.

Self-confidence and Self-esteem: Effective practice: 30–50 months

Ensure that key practitioners offer extra support to children in new situations.

This is a transition that many children will face. Use the same strategies as mentioned above for moving school if the children are moving *to* a new house, nearby or at a distance. When you receive new children who have moved *in*, especially part-way through the term, when friendships have been established, you will have to be more proactive.

Actions to take when moving to a new area or town:

● Follow your normal induction process as far as possible.

● Try to set up some visits before the actual start day.

● Children could draw or write some welcome cards and send them to the new address for the child to find on moving-in day.

● Have a label for his coat peg, etc. in place before the child's first visit so that he sees that you are expecting him.

TOP TIP!

To help a child who has moved into your area, a buddy is a good approach to start the settling-in process:

It gives the child a person to play with, someone who will show them where things are kept.

Maybe the mother will also befriend the new mum and invite her and the child to visit.

Choose the buddy by their temperament – someone who is confident but kind and caring.

> *It is also worth checking addresses. Don't give details away, but if you can match the new child to someone who lives close by, then they may see each other on the way in or going home, or playing locally during the weekends or holidays.*

The challenges of learning

The young child is a great questioner. Their seemingly endless 'Why?' or 'How?' can sometimes irritate adults. For you, it should be a signal of an enquiring mind, of a child who is thinking, who wants to know and who is ready to listen, to experiment and to find out. This is the kind of behaviour that you want to encourage, so the quality and tone of your response is going to be important. It is going to give the child the message that you are there for him, that you are pleased that he wants to know more, and that this is a place where learning and enquiry are valued.

Responding to questions

The way that you respond to questions will encourage or discourage the child from developing a love of learning.

Reflecting on practice

What if?

Younger children tend to ask 'what' questions, but you should be expecting more 'why' questions from your older or more able children. Monitor the sorts of questions that your children ask.

One way to work towards this is to encourage the children to ask 'What if?' Spend some time encouraging them to respond to apparently wild statements or off-the-wall ideas. For example:

What if a cat had wings?

What if you could only eat food that was yellow?

What if you met a lion in the car park?

What if you were invisible?

What if your baby brother could run faster than you?

What if everyone in the world looked exactly the same?

TOP TIP!

Some useful responses are:

What do you think?

What an interesting idea.

Have you got a suggestion that you've already thought about?

I'm not sure about that. Shall we see if we can find something about it in a book?

Do you know, I'd never thought of that. But now you mention it I think that ...

Do you remember when we looked at those spiders in the garden the other day? Can you remember what we said about the way that they ...?

That reminds me of ... Were you thinking of that or did you have another idea?

- Never forget that your aim is to help the child to think and to understand.

- Enter into a discussion that provides additional information, and so help the child's thinking to progress. By adding to the child's existing knowledge through discussion you are helping him think more accurately and probe more deeply.

- Encourage your children to ask questions that have no answers but stimulate debate.

- Try to stimulate further thinking, not inhibit it. Statements such as 'Because it is' or 'You know that, don't keep on about it' have no place in a learning environment.

- Stimulate the child to go a step further in his thinking by asking additional questions.

- Expressing your thoughts is not as simple as it sounds. Children need opportunities to explain their reasoning. Plan some activities that encourage questioning and discussion. Remind the children that there may not be a 'right' answer. For example:

Activity:

Pose a scenario.

Describe three different responses or reactions.

Encourage the children to express their opinion.

Scenario: Three children are playing football in the park. The ball goes over the railings into a field.

Responses: Jason wants to climb over the railings to get the ball.

> *Andi wants to go home and explain to his mum that he has lost his new football.*

> *Katie wants to go and ask the man sitting on the bench if he can get the ball back for them.*

Suggested questions:

What would you do?

Was Andi right?

What might happen when he did this?

Why do you think this one (i.e. the child's own choice) was a good idea?

Why do you think this wasn't the best thing to do?

Are any of these dangerous things to do?

Might the children get hurt?

What if the man on the bench was Katie's grandpa?

Is it more important to get your football or to be safe?

Self-confidence and Self-esteem: Developing matters: 40–60+ months

Have a developing awareness of their own needs, views and feelings, and be sensitive to the needs, views and feelings of others.

Reflecting on practice

Beyond the box? Scary!

Children who lack self-confidence may be frightened of going beyond the box even if it is just thinking.

Let them experience the positive responses that happen when someone else's thoughts are brought out into the open for general discussion.

They could engage in a discussion with a friend. Ask all of the children to tell their answer or thoughts to the child sitting next to them. Practising saying the words in this more private way can help children to work out their

→

response, find the right words, and experience someone else's reaction to their ideas, before they have to speak in the larger group.

Consider the following:

How could you take steps to encourage discussion and high-level thinking?

You could investigate some of the thinking programmes that are around. These would help all of your children, not just the hesitant ones. You could try 'philosophy for children': www.p4c.com

High expectations

Professionals often use expressions such as 'wanting the children to do their best' or 'achieving their full potential' to state the aims of their educational setting. This can refer to behaviour just as much as learning. But what does this mean in practice?

Why not try this?

'We have high expectations of our children'

Think about this statement in reference to behaviour. Here are the views of some practitioners about the way that they encourage their children to behave well. Debate these examples with your colleagues:

> The children take their cue from me. If I expect them to behave and show that expectation in my body language and in the words I use, then they usu-ally manage to behave really well. This happened last Wednesday when we went out for a visit to the art gallery. They all behaved so well and I was very proud of them.

The teacher was also on show to the world at large.

Do you think this would have affected her own behaviour and the way she responded to the children?

> I encourage the children to take a lot of responsibility for their day, for example they can choose when to have their snack. They also can choose when to work outdoors. But if there are any arguments then they have to come in. I step straight in and make sure there's no unpleasantness.

Is there a connection between the amount of responsibility you give the children for their work and play, and the level of responsibility you encourage them to take for their behaviour and relationships?

→

What messages are the children getting if there is a discrepancy between the two?

> I think it's very important that children learn how to get on with other people. All of our children have a working partner for when we have to do something with a partner. I sort out the pairs at the beginning of the term and then they always know who to work with and there's no time wasted at the start of the activity when you have to ask them to find a partner.

What are these children learning about relationships?

What message are they getting about their ability to form friendships?

What value is placed on their social skills?

- Is it possible to carry out high expectations for behaviour in your setting?
- Are there any changes that would have to happen in the way your setting is organised, or in the culture and ethos of your setting?

Developing a professional Code of Conduct within the setting

It doesn't matter how knowledgeable you are about the EYFS or the Key Stage 1 curriculum, or how organised your records are – there has to be another dimension to your professional role. You have to enjoy being with the children. You also have to behave in such a way that the children know that you enjoy being with them.

I have worked in many different settings, and on leaving them have listened to words of thanks from staff and parents. The one that stays with me came from a seven-year-old girl who thanked me for 'always putting the learning into our fun'. I wanted to punch the air with pride!

Without losing your dignity or respect you should be able to have a relationship with the children that includes having fun.

Reflecting on practice

Steph, Early Years practitioner

A group of four year olds had decided to use some long lengths of guttering as a race track for their small cars. How fast could they go?

Would they go faster if the slope was longer, or steeper? They couldn't fix the guttering up as high as they wanted it to be. An adult was needed to act as a support. Steph was the practitioner working outdoors that afternoon. It was really time to pack things away; she was just starting to do this when the group approached her, full of enthusiasm and involvement in their task. She hesitated for a moment, conscious of her 'duty', but when she registered the children's eagerness, and the learning that was happening for them as they started to understand ramps and inclines and other scientific knowledge, as well as their commitment to the task, and the investigative way they were approaching this problem, she chose to help them. These four year olds will respect this adult who showed how much she understood them and was willing to help them.

Consider the following:

How would you have responded in Steph's position? In your setting are you encouraged to respond to the children in this way or are you tied to the timetable and learning plan so tightly that the children's needs and enthusiasm are pushed aside?

- Be sensitive to their moods and respond accordingly.

- Don't laugh at their efforts to explain things.

- Share their joy when they achieve.

- Play with them in their role play. Consider this example: Sarah, aged four, dressed in all her finery, with a large hat and a long skirt, interrupted the teacher as she was working with another group of children on their measuring. 'Can you just tell this cat to drink its milk up?' was the exasperated request. 'Drink that milk up, like a good cat,' said the teacher to the toy cat that Sarah was holding out to her.

- Try to see things from their point of view, entering into their 'good ideas'. Again, an example of how you might do this: Doreen was working in a nursery setting. She was playing with the children in the role-play area, which was set up as a hospital. It was her turn to be the patient and she was lying on the camp bed, with a large bandage round her head and her right arm in a sling. Danni was in the process of covering most of her leg in another bandage. Up came three-year-old Mia, clutching her copy of 'The Enormous Crocodile' or, as she called it, 'The Enormous Cockledile', her absolute favourite story at the moment. 'While you're just lying there you might as well read this to me,' she announced and sat down by the bed. So, Doreen read.

Young children won't judge you as silly if you are still wearing your feathery hat as you supervise the painting. They will be thrilled when you skip with them or join in the dancing. Don't be afraid to pull a funny face, or use a strange voice when the story you are reading to them suggests it. In other words – have fun with the children!

In touch with parents – keeping it positive

It is very easy to assume that you know more than the parents about the right way to raise and educate children. You may be an expert on children and their development and learning, but each parent is an expert on their own child. Never underestimate the level of a parent's knowledge or ability. Never assume that you know all about them and their personal, family or business situation and commitments.

Try to understand their situation

Mother of four/corporate boss: 'Yes, you're right. I have been neglecting his reading lately. I'll try and find a window where I can fit him in.'

What is your reaction to this?

- Is she a mother who is neglecting her son?

- Is she simply using the language with which she is most familiar?

- Is she so stressed that one more demand on her time may be her downfall?

You may not like the way she approaches this but she is finding a solution in her own way. Think of ways that you could help her to manage the time she can spare to make it as productive as possible.

Try to turn the negative into the positive

If you have to face a confrontation with a parent make it your aim to part on a positive note, even if you don't start there:

Sometimes worry is expressed as anger. Many parents have bad memories of school or authority and they have to work themselves up in order to even come through the door. Their worries then burst out and can easily be misinterpreted as anger. Reading between the lines is important. Here are some simple steps you can take to calm the situation down, and resume a peaceful partnership with your parents.

- Don't react instantly.

- Let their anger burn out as they rant.

● When they stop, ask them to join you sitting somewhere. It might even be appropriate to put the kettle on.

● Now ask them to tell you it again, so that you can make notes about their problem. This time they will probably tell you in a calmer way, a more orderly way, and you can start to work together on finding a resolution to their problem – real or perceived.

● Read your notes back to them, and ask them if they agree with your interpretation. Suggest some responses that you are prepared to make. Decide upon some steps that they may be willing to make. Sign the notes as your agreement as to the actions you will all take.

● Decide on a date when you will all get together again to check on progress.

● Shake hands, thank them for letting you know about the situation and for the help they are going to give as you work together to put things right.

Try to get to know them

Whenever you have to deal with parents it is made much easier if you can find a connection with them. Look at this example of one mother and her relationship with the school.

Reflecting on practice

Liam and his mum

Liam's first teacher was young and newly qualified. Liam's mum came in often to complain about his scuffed new shoes, his missing PE shorts, the sweat-shirt he'd left behind yesterday and so on and on. It was constant. The young teacher dreaded her approach and met the accusations with defensive words.

Liam's next teacher was older, with more years of experience in school, and children of her own. Liam's mum came in, full of bluster and pent-up anger. 'I want to talk to you about the hole in the knee of Liam's new trousers.' 'Oh! Don't talk to me about boys and trousers,' replied the teacher in a weary tone. 'One of mine went through three pairs in one day once. He said it was because he *had* to hide behind the wall as that was the best hiding place!' Teacher and parent went on to talk about the difficulties of raising boys compared to their older children who were girls. They had found a common ground. By the end of that term the mother had confided that she couldn't actually read or spell very well and that she was terrified of coming into school and talking with the teachers. Eventually she started to come in for an hour each week to help with art and design.

Don't be afraid to meet your parents in this way. You have to remain detached and professional, but that doesn't preclude showing that you understand them. It wouldn't be appropriate to tell them about your personal relationships or anxieties, for example, but you can let them know that you too are human. The children are often amazed to see you in the street on a Saturday, as many of them think you live in the school or nursery. Parents of course don't hold this belief but they can still have misconceptions about you. At the end of the school year one infant school teacher was asked, 'When will you be allowed to go up to the Juniors?'

Having a good relationship with parents is the base on which you can develop a dialogue with your parents, and so establish the partnership that brings the children a sense of continuity and security in their lives.

Conclusion

Life is full of problems or challenges – it depends on how you view them. Many problems can be solved if you think them through. Challenges can be exciting opportunities. You want your children to have an optimistic view on life, believing that they can overcome the hard times. You don't want them to be so overwhelmed that they spend their life avoiding situations or hiding from the world. To achieve this positive state of mind you can help the children to cope with the difficult things, supporting them when they are in need, and you can start to develop in them the skills to deal with life.

Key ideas summary

You now know that if you want to help your children to develop a positive approach to life you have to:

- Encourage their sense of self.

- Help them to learn how to tackle problems.

- Be ready to support them through stressful situations.

- Respond positively to their questions and sense of curiosity.

- Have high expectations of their behaviour and social skills.

- Have fun.

Going further

Useful websites for finding out more information and available support systems:

Bereavement: www.winstonswish.org.uk
　　　　　　　www.childbereavement.org.uk

Parents in prison: www.ormiston.org.uk

Separation and divorce: www.itsnotyourfault.org.uk

Squirrel says

It was a sad day at Warren Buildings. Overnight someone had been in the children's play area and smashed it all up. The climbing frame had been smeared with green paint. The slide had been scraped and scratched so that you couldn't slide smoothly down it any more. The grass was covered in glass, and one of the wooden slats that made up the bench had been removed.

The children and their parents were standing round looking.

'Keep off the grass,' warned Mrs Rabbit. 'You don't want to get cut by the glass.'

Squirrel saw the group when he came out of the main door to go to the shop for his newspaper.

'Whatever's happened here?' he asked.

'Vandals,' said Mr Weasel.

'Naughty people,' said Fergus Ferret.

'Well,' said Squirrel. 'What are we going to do about it? It's only a mess. If we all help we'll soon sort it out and the children will be able to play again, and old Grandpa Mouse will be able to sit on the bench and watch the world go by.'

Everyone thought it was a good idea.

Mr Ferret brought his big pot of blue paint and started to paint over the green splashes on the climbing frame. It soon looked great in its new colour.

Mrs Rabbit and Mrs Weasel found some very thick gloves and started picking up all the pieces of glass from the grass and putting them into a bucket. →

William, the eldest Weasel, knew where to find a piece of wood that would fit the bench, and Mrs Ferret fetched a screwdriver and four shiny screws so that she could replace the missing slat on the bench.

Squirrel went to ask Grandpa Mouse if he had a plane so that they could smooth the slide, and then went and made some big jugs of juice for the children. Mrs Vole heard all the noise and came along with mugs of coffee for the grown-ups and a big plate of cookies for everyone to share.

Squirrel says,

'If everyone helps then you can soon sort out a problem.'

From policy to practice

What this chapter will explore:

- How the children can participate in the creation of your behaviour policy
- Ways to help the children understand your policy for behaviour and how it applies to them every day
- Planning for behaviour development and learning, linking your behaviour policy with the requirements of the PSE aspect of the EYFS

The first eight chapters of this book have helped you to explore the various processes of development and learning that have to happen if children are to become more socially competent. You have found out about some of the skills and strategies you can use with young children as you help them to grow in self-respect and emotional well-being, ready to take full advantage of the learning and education you offer them. In this chapter there will be a focus on the practical application of this, as you first of all apply this knowledge of child development and child psychology to your setting's behaviour policy, and then as you bring that policy to life in your day-to-day interactions with the children.

As members of the learning community your children have to be able to take advantage of all the exciting and instructive opportunities that you will be planning for them. They have to be able to listen, think and apply their learning. This can only happen when you have created the right sort of atmosphere for learning to happen, and that includes how you manage the children's behaviour so that they are ready and able to play their part.

Your setting will have a behaviour policy, but what matters is whether you use that policy to your advantage. You can use it in a variety of ways:

- as a framework in which to set the children's personal and social education;
- as a guide to the level of politeness and good manners that you will expect of the children;
- to define your own behaviour as you model the kind of behaviour that you want the children to show.

Your behaviour policy

Appendix 1 contains some ideas for setting out your policy, and for ways to share it with others. You will find some formats you can use on the website: www.pearsoned.co.uk/essentialguides.

Children need to feel involved. Just like adults, when they have a sense of ownership about things, they will be more motivated to support and maintain these systems, rules or routines than they would if they have simply been imposed on them. You know that the same rules will apply each year, but if you have discussed them with these particular children, and used their own wording to write them up, then they will have the sense that they actually decided on them, and that they belong to them. They are more likely to follow the rules that they created and show more respect for the values that they determined to be important.

Can children enter into a debate at this level? Can they persuade their friends about what rules, routines or values should be part of the way of life in your setting? Well, these are the people who can find ten reasons for not going to bed yet, or for not eating their greens! Of course they can come up with lots of persuasive arguments and lateral thoughts if they are sufficiently interested in affecting the situation. You have to be prepared to hear some strange or bizarre ideas, but you can always find sensitive ways to help the children see the practicality – or not – of things. One group of children were discussing ways to prevent children trampling on the plants at the edge of the garden they had made. Suggestions included a moat and an armed guard! Eventually a more practical solution was dreamed up and they all enjoyed planting up some wooden tubs to act as visual reminders of the end of the play area and the start of the garden.

The children's contribution

It is quite likely that your policy has been written by adults and that it is known to the adults. What about the children? Are there any ways in which you can include them in the process? Some of your children may be old enough to play a small part in the creation of some aspects of the policy itself.

- Involving the children wherever possible in the formation of the policy could be one of the statements contained within it.

- You can certainly give children the opportunity to think about rules and routines and why they have to exist. Chapters 1 and 2 have more about this.

- Some schools include even the youngest of their children as class representatives on their school council. They are supported in learning how to join in with the discussion and take ideas and decisions back to share with their classmates.

- Spend some time at the start of each term talking with the children about how they need to behave so that everyone can be happy. Talk about what makes them happy and, conversely, what makes them unhappy, uncomfortable or sad.

- Discuss all the ideas that the children suggest. Help them to refine their ideas and then, when you write up the statements, use the same words and sentence structure where possible to help those who are starting to read to recognise the words. Making it positive will help to create a positive atmosphere, where everyone is thinking about what they should be doing, not concentrating on the negative. Appendix 1 and the website www.pearsoned .co.uk/essentialguides contain ideas for formats you could use.

> **TOP TIP!**
>
> *Add pictures to show each of these 'rules' in action so that all of the children can understand what is written there. The children can contribute to this.*

Bringing your policy to life for the children

Through stories

Throughout this book, and on the website, there are simple stories about Squirrel and his friends that you can use with the children to explain what is meant by specific aspects of the policy. They can be part of your planned PSE programme or they can be used to start a discussion when some behaviour is causing you some problems. Putting the message into a context that the children will understand helps them to make sense of things. This is especially useful when you are dealing with abstract concepts such as sharing or being kind.

The stories included here are based on animal characters because these are non-threatening to children, and it avoids anything that could be construed as talking about a particular child or family. The stories are set in a high-rise block of flats to create the sense of a community trying to look after its members. They are very much intended as a starting point for you to adapt or modify to suit the needs of your children. You could tell the stories with other characters, or move them into a village if that's more representative of your children's home life. Try turning them into aliens or sea creatures, jungle animals or fairies, each in their own environment. Your imagination will inspire you to adapt the ideas.

Through practice

Plan to allow some time at the start of the new school year when you can focus on the routines that you have in place. Look at the PSE section of the Early Years Foundation Stage. In the aspect 'Making Relationships', one of the Early Learning Goals is:

> 'Work as part of a group or class, taking turns, and sharing fairly, understanding that there needs to be agreed values and codes of behaviour for groups of people, including adults and children, to work together harmoniously.'

This can be the focus ELG for your PSE work at this point, so that you are able to concentrate on helping the children settle into this new setting, familiarising themselves with all that is expected of them.

- Children can help you to make the labels for their coat-pegs and drawers so that they will know where to keep their personal things. This helps them with their self-confidence.

- Encourage independence by finding a way for the children to self-register at the start of each session.

TOP TIP!

The child's name can be written on a card that can be tucked in behind the name card on their coat-peg. On entry they can remove their card and place it on a special board – attached by Velcro® or slipped through some elastic stretched over an interesting fabric – as a sign that they are present. At the end of the session they can replace their name card behind their coat-peg label.

- Allow time for the children to put all their belongings away in the proper places. Help them to do this. Check that everything is where it should be. This gives the children confidence in their ability to operate independently. Praise them when they get things all sorted out and the cloakroom areas are tidy. In the same way, give plenty of time for children to collect things up at the end of the session. If you are in school, allow time before and after playtimes for children to manage their own coats.

- Plan PSE sessions when you can all talk about the routines that you have: discuss why there is a rule about only four in the sand, or wearing aprons to paint; explain why it is important that children let you know that they are going out of the room to use the toilet; share ideas on how you can remember where all the equipment or resources are kept.

TOP TIP!

Attach some pegs to a solid board so that they can be opened where they are – or use large brightly coloured bull-dog clips. In a box nearby, place small name cards – one for each child. There should be the same number of pegs as you have toilets, or as you would want children to be out of the room at the same time. If a child leaves the room he finds his own name card and fixes it in the peg. If the pegs are full, he has to wait. On returning he takes his card out and replaces it in the box. This means that children can be independent but also responsible. And you will know where everyone is.

All of these are steps towards developing children's self-esteem as they start to see that their opinion matters and that your aim is to make them comfortable and at ease in these new surroundings. They are also a step towards independence.

Planning to teach your behaviour policy

The focus throughout this book is that you have to be proactive, and be prepared to actually teach children how to behave as well as supporting their developing abilities in sorting out what is and what isn't acceptable in their particular society. If you have a behaviour policy which describes the sorts of behaviour that you want the children to use, then you should be looking for opportunities each day when you can actively teach these skills and strategies, or when you can point out and praise your children's positive behaviours.

When you are planning your activities for the PSE aspect of the EYFS use this book to suggest some of the themes you might take, and some of the activities that might be included.

Cooperating

> **Making Relationships: Development matters: 22–36 months**
>
> Seek out others to share experiences.

- Make some labels to encourage sharing of resources, for example:
  - A picture of two children throwing and catching a ball to put up near the basket of balls outdoors.
  - 'Has your friend got enough dough?' to put near the table with the dough/clay, etc. on it.
- Play some ring games in which children need to share or cooperate, for example:
  - Roll a ball to someone in the circle, saying their name as you do so. They reply 'thank you' and say your name before passing it on to another child.
  - Two children stand holding hands together, up high to make an arch. The others pass under the arch as they dance round in a ring. When the music stops the child under the arch chooses a friend to make a second arch. The game continues until there are too many arches and not enough children left in the ring. Start again with children who have not yet had a turn as the arch.
- Set up a party theme in your role-play area with invitations, party 'food' and present wrapping.
- Team building games are suggested in Chapter 8.
- Read *The Doorbell Rang* by Pat Hutchins and make your own biscuits to share.
- Tell a story together. You start and the children take it in turns to add the next line. Start by retelling a familiar tale and work up to a point where you can create a story all of your own.

TOP TIP!

If you have a very shy child, seat him to your left in the circle, and start telling the story with the child to your right. The shy child will therefore be last and you can remind him that lots of stories end with the special story words 'And they all lived happily ever after'.

Friendship

Making Relationships: Development matters: 30–50 months

Form friendships with other children.

- Read *The Rainbow Fish* by Marcus Pfister and enact the story, then talk about being friends and what that entails.
- Provide a selection of cards, postcards, paper and envelopes, set up a post box and encourage the children to communicate with their friends in this way.
- Games with partners are suggested in Chapter 4.
- Make Valentine's Day a special day about friendship, for example:
  - Make heart-shaped biscuits.
  - Make a heart-shaped card using red collage materials and give it to your friend.
  - Cut heart shapes from red paper and use as place mats for snack time.

Being special

Self-confidence and Self-esteem: Development matters: 22–36 months

Feel pride in their own achievements.

- Link with a theme on babies or families.
- Read *Something Special* by Nicola Moon and make a collection of special things – or photos of your special things.

- Talk about what makes us all special in PSE or Circle Time (see Chapter 3).

- Collect self-portraits, paintings, photographs or collages, and make a display labelled 'We are special'.

- Have a magnetic board labelled 'This is my special day'. Attach a photo or name for a child or staff member having a birthday or other event worth cele- brating. Have other traditions that you follow for everyone's special day – a cake, candles, a song, a special chair for lunch, snack or story time.

- Write every child's name and date of birth on individual cards. Don't forget to check for any religious or cultural reasons why some families may not want their children to be included in this. Place the cards in a box in date order. Decorate the box so that it looks appealing to young children, perhaps with a party theme of balloons or party hats. Every day check the box. The name at the front should be today's birthday child. At the end of the day that card goes to the back of the pile. This means you'll never miss anyone out. Add new children if they start during the year. Write the names boldly and place the box where it can be seen by the children. There will be eager anticipation of 'Tomorrow my name will at the front.' Have a blank card to cover up the name if there is no birthday today.

Being me

> ### Sense of Community: Development matters: 40–60+ months
> Have a positive self-image, and show that they are comfortable with themselves.

- Create a grid of string or cord in a frame ready for weaving. As an alternative, you could use something that lends itself to being a base for weaving, such as a tennis racquet, an old bicycle wheel, a large garden sieve, or a length of plastic-coated wire mesh from a garden centre. Everyone chooses a length of ribbon, a strip of fabric, some thick wool or cord and tells the others why they chose it. It should 'say' something about the child. They each weave it somewhere – at random – into the mesh. Children should remember where their piece is. During Circle Time they can pass the weaving round and tell their friends all about their own piece.

  - 'That's me. I'm the red ribbon because I like Liverpool.'

  - 'That green ribbon is mine. It's the same colour as my Grandad's house, and I love going there to stay.'

- Draw round a child, and then go over the line in a bold coloured marker pen. The child can add his own face/features and write his name outside of the figure. He then sticks on to the figure things that are all about him. He can cut out pictures of his favourite toys and foods that he likes and stick them on. He can add photos of people or pets who are special to him – parents may be willing to bring in a picture that can be photocopied or an extra print from a digital camera. He could copy a drawing from his favourite book to stick on. Add his hand prints using paint in a colour of his choice.

- There are a number of activities in Chapter 6 to help the children recognise their own individuality.

Being different

> ### Sense of Community: Development matters: 40–60+ months
>
> Understand that people have different needs, views, cultures and beliefs which need to be treated with respect.

- There are ideas in Chapter 3 dealing with diversity and difference.
- Celebrate as many different festivals as you can. Don't limit yourself to just the ones that your children will share with their families.
- You can find different ways of celebrating the same sort of event, such as:
  - Light in dark days: Diwali, St Lucia's Day, Christmas, Hannukah.

If you deal with them as a group then you can start to explain about similarities as well as differences. Point out that the same sorts of things are important to all people even if they choose to celebrate them in different ways. Harvest, new babies and the New Year could also be treated this way.

When children know that all sorts of people and lifestyles are accepted in society then they can be open about their own differences. They don't have to be afraid of the opinion of others. Theoretically, it should inhibit the potential bully. Bullying tends to be one person searching out someone's weak spot or difference and mocking it.

Truth and trust

> ### Behaviour and Self-control: Development matters: 22–36 months
>
> Are aware that some actions can hurt or harm others.

- Chapter 2 includes some discussion on reasons why children may not always tell the truth. Be alert for these reasons and treat them seriously.

- Tell the children the story of *The Boy Who Cried Wolf*. Why did people not believe him when there really was a wolf? What could he have done differently? Talk about the importance of people being able to trust you to tell the truth.

- The children may be familiar with the story of Pinocchio and how his wooden nose grew longer every time he said something that wasn't true. Use some dough to make a pretend nose for one of your dolls. Choose a child to make the doll say something. The others have to guess – was it true or false? If it is false, the one who guessed correctly can add some more dough to make the nose a little longer. If it actually was true then the child at the front gets another turn.

- Demonstrate your trust for the children by giving them real money when they are playing in the shop. Counting it before and after they have played with it to check that it is all there is good counting practice. Explain to the children that this is what happens in shops – the shopkeeper counts the money into the till in the morning ready to give change to his customers. At night he counts it again and puts it aside ready for tomorrow. The loss of a few coins should be treated in the same way as the loss of some pieces from a jigsaw puzzle – their loss affects the next person to play.

TOP TIP!

With younger children use all the same coins to make the counting easier. Older children might be able to count up coins in different denominations.

Telling the truth is a sign of the respect you have for other people. It also demonstrates a desire to be part of the group and to be accepted and trusted. Scientists investigating trust, in biological and psychological terms, found that the more you trust someone the more they tended to trust you (Martin, 2006, p 82).

Talking about emotions

Self-confidence and Self-esteem: Development matters: 40–60+ months

Express needs and feelings in appropriate ways.

- There are a lot of ideas in Chapter 5 for encouraging the children to talk about their emotions.

- Collect pictures cut from magazines or cards that show different emotions. Laminate them if you want to use them more than once. Children could sort them into happy and sad. They might then be able to subdivide them into more precise definitions. Try: someone who is amused, someone who is scared, someone who is nervous. How do they know? What are they noticing?

- Dance to some music. When it stops you call out an emotion – 'sad', 'frightened', 'amazed', and so on – and the children have to make that face or adopt that posture. Ask one or two children what might make them look like this. Don't linger too long on the questioning, keep the game going.

- Lay some large sheets of coloured paper out, perhaps one to a table around the room. On each one write the name of a feeling in large letters – maybe just an outline so that the children can colour them in. Try: sad, happy, scared, Some children may be ready to try more specific emotions, such as ecstatic, amazed, terrified, shocked. Children can cut out faces that show these feelings, or draw things, people or events that cause them to feel like this. They stick their offerings on any of the labelled sheets as they wish.

Talking about their emotions is a basic requirement if children are to let you know when things are going wrong for them. Keep introducing new words to help them to be more precise.

Reflecting on practice

A Good Childhood

Over 18 months of 2007 and 2008 a panel met to discuss the place and the needs of children in today's society. The Good Childhood Inquiry was set up by The Children's Society, which is based in the Church of England. One of the seven themes that the Inquiry explored was education, led by Kathy Sylva, the well-known professor of educational psychology at the University of Oxford. Her findings and those of the others on the panel are collated in *A Good Childhood* (Layard and Dunn, 2009).

One of the findings was that most of the teachers surveyed were concerned about 'low-level disruption and impoliteness'. The two suggested solutions, both of equal importance, were that:

Schools should be 'values-based communities', where everybody shows respect for everybody else – the children, the parents, the staff.

Schools should 'help pupils to manage their emotions'.

Consider the following:

1. Which values are held by your setting? Are they transparent within your behaviour policy and practice?

2. What systems do you have for helping your children to manage their emotions? Do you have additional support available for those children experiencing difficulty in this area of development?

Conclusion

This chapter has helped you to visualise how you can make your behaviour policy something much more than a dull piece of paper written and maintained by adults. It has shown you how you can use the policy as a guide to some of the planning that you will be doing, especially at the start of the year when you are trying to settle children into the routines of your setting, and as you work towards creating the sort of working environment you want.

Key ideas summary

You now know how to bring your policy to life by:

● Involving your children in the formation of some of the rules and routines of your setting.

● Finding ways to remind children of those rules.

● Telling stories to provide concrete examples of the rules.

● Including some of the rules or routines in your planned teaching so that children have a chance to remember how to behave in the setting and beyond.

Going further

You may want to find out more about school councils and whether such a system would be appropriate in your setting. To do this you could look at the following two websites:

www.schoolcouncils.org – School Councils UK

This site has practical information on how to organise and manage a school council. This is aimed mainly at slightly older children, primary and secondary, but the broad aims can be adapted to suit the needs of younger children.

www.teachers.tv/series/school-councils

This site includes a useful video clip (*Starting Early*) describing how one school, Farnborough Grange Infant and Nursery School, in Farnborough, Hampshire, includes their Reception class children and how they make the whole experience a manageable and productive one.

There are also links to other useful videos for Early Years.

Conclusion

'The human baby is the most socially influenced creature on earth.'

'How one person behaves affects how another behaves and his or her behaviour then influences the original person in a circular process.'

(Gerhardt, 2004, pp 10 and 9)

Your part in this process is to take charge, to understand the baby and the young child, and to respond to them in positive ways that will shape their behaviour, so that they in turn are able to behave in acceptable ways which will positively affect their own society.

Appendix 1

WRITING A BEHAVIOUR POLICY

Broad guidelines for writing any policy document

- A policy should be created in discussion with all those who will be involved in carrying it out.
- A policy should be easy to read, clear and concise. If people can interpret it in different ways you may end up with problems.
- A policy should be a framework for the actions that you will take.

Before you start to put this policy together try to determine for yourself what *you* mean by behaviour. Here is one definition you could use:

Behaviour is the way we act and respond to people and to situations we find ourselves in.

You may want to discuss this with your colleagues and then write your own definition.

As you discuss and write this policy remember that although it will contain an outline of the sanctions and rewards you will use to encourage positive behaviour, it is much more than a policy for ways to discipline children. This policy is about how you will take the children from where they are now, and help them to learn and maintain acceptable patterns of behaviour.

Throughout this book you have considered the processes that help a child to develop the skills he needs if he is to behave in age-appropriate and setting-appropriate ways. These processes will be brought to life as you carry out your setting's policy for behaviour management.

'Providers must have an effective behaviour management policy which is adhered to by all members of staff.'

(DfES, 2007, Non-statutory Guidance, p 28)

Deciding on the sections in your behaviour policy

A simple way to start creating this policy is to consider the following questions:

- What do we hope to achieve by having this policy for behaviour?
- How will we go about achieving these goals?
- What behaviour do we want to see in our setting?
- What will we do if we see behaviour that we want?
- What behaviour do we not accept in our setting?
- What will we do if we see behaviour that we don't want?
- Are there any regulations or laws that we have to follow?
- Are there any people outside of the setting who will be able to help us to achieve our aims?
- What should parents do if they are not happy with any actions we take?

Here are some notes about each of these questions. Read through them and think about them in relation to the situation at your setting.

What do we hope to achieve by having this policy?

This is the ultimate aim of your behaviour policy. It is about the standard of behaviour you would like to see. Not everyone will be displaying this standard, and even those who in general have attained this level of behaviour may have days when they don't manage to keep to it. It describes the perfect situation that you are all striving for.

How will we go about achieving these goals?

This is about the expectations you have of the adults as they help the children to achieve these standards of behaviour.

- The adults' own behaviour will be a model for the children to copy.
- Think about the way that adults intervene and respond to children's behaviour – positive or not.
- Will there be any direct teaching and where will this fit into your curriculum plans?
- Consider the rules and routines that you will have for supporting the children's efforts to behave and how staff will put them into effect.

What behaviour do we want to see in our setting?

Describe the sort of behaviour you want to see from the children and the adults. Be positive in this section. As you have read this book you will have found that there are behaviours linked to social conventions, to moral attitudes, to developing emotional competence and self-esteem, as well as those behaviours which directly affect the children's ability to learn. Try to cover all aspects of behaviour in your initial thinking, and then find ways to express them succinctly.

What will we do if we see behaviour that we want?

Part of the important work of early education is to help the children move from being egocentric to recognising that others have feelings and rights, and recognising that we should all respect each other. This is set out in the PSE curriculum and should be reinforced throughout the day.

It is important that all staff and adults helping in the setting remember to reinforce good behaviour by:

Acknowledging it: 'I noticed Sam helping James pick up the pot of buttons he's just dropped.'

Praising it: 'Well done for helping put those books way, Nasim.'

Rewarding it: 'This group have played so well together that they can sit on the bean bags for story time.'

Children are often told what they have done wrong, but are rarely told exactly what they did that was right. Your policy is a place where you can set down the responsibility of all staff to do this.

What behaviour do we not accept in our setting?

This is the place where you can think of the negative aspects of behaviour that you might see and that you won't accept. Again, think of all aspects of behaviour as detailed above. As you discuss this, try to think about why you don't like these particular behaviours. Make rational decisions about why you won't accept this behaviour. You will probably find that at some level they all cause hurt or distress to another person.

What will we do if we see behaviour that we don't want?

It is most important to remember that you are dealing with very young children. Their level of maturity may be affecting the behaviour they show, or their ability to understand your response. Always be ready to take this into account as you deal with children. Make the consequences suit the age of the child as well as the nature of the action.

It is your responsibility to correct the children when they get it wrong, but more in a sense of making them think, helping them to see alternative ways of responding and reminding them over several occasions about it, rather than giving a strict 'punishment'.

The children may see certain types of behaviour at home, and as fast as you are demonstrating one way to handle a situation they are experiencing another with their family. For this reason you should include in your policy the point at which you will inform the parents about the unacceptable behaviour and talk to them about approaches they can make at home, ways that match what you are doing.

This is the place where you can describe the sanctions you will take, when that becomes a necessary course of action. It should include how you will deal with adults who behave in unacceptable ways, as well as describing how you will deal with the children. Sanctions should develop:

On the first occasion we will …

If the behaviour is repeated that same day we will …

If the behaviour continues we will …

Think about the way that adults are dealt with at work: a verbal warning, a written warning, three written warnings and you're out! Or some such pattern. Or think about footballers, and the yellow and red card systems.

Exclusion needs to be mentioned here, but the details will be set out in a separate policy. Refer the reader to this policy.

Are there any regulations or laws that we have to follow?

You may have rules and regulations that you have to follow. Use this opportunity to remind all the staff about them. There are guidelines related to safeguarding children, handling children and the *Every Child Matters* agenda, as well as Standards and Guidance for the EYFS and the criteria that Ofsted will use in their assessment of the setting.

You may have children from racial or religious backgrounds who would find some particular behaviours offensive. Find out about these and make sure everyone is aware of them.

Are there any people outside of the setting who will be able to help us to achieve our aims?

If you have children who display behaviour that is especially difficult, threatening or uncontrollable, you will need to seek outside help. Who can you contact and for what purpose? List them by profession and contact number. People change jobs so don't rely on personal names when you write up your list.

You may want to investigate the possibility of having some professional development on this, and you could identify those who can provide this service for you.

Complaints and compliments

What should parents do if they are not happy with any actions we take?

Any policy should include a simple statement referring parents or other adults to the complaints procedure you have in place.

What should parents do if they like the actions we take?

Parents who are pleased with the way that you manage their child's behaviour should be invited to write down their comments, which can be kept as evidence of the good work you are doing with the children.

What happens to the policy after we've written it?

The last line of the policy should be the date that it was signed and accepted, and the date when it will be reviewed. Don't forget to put this date in the diary at the same time so that it doesn't get overlooked. Ideally this should be done at the start of every school year. Sit together as a staff team and read it out loud, paragraph by paragraph, inviting discussion or clarification. Ask questions such as, 'Did this work?' or 'Could this be done differently to improve ...?' This means that you will have reviewed it and informed all of your staff about it at one sitting.

As you think about each of these questions remember: this policy applies to children and adults alike. All staff and any parents or visitors on the premises will also be expected to keep to the policy. It is therefore important that you think about how you will keep everyone informed.

You should include a copy of this policy in your prospectus or handbook, or in the pack you give to new parents. They have two choices: they can accept your policy or they can take their child to another setting. If they know about it in advance of registering their child with you then you can refer to it should they ever complain about the way that you respond to their child's behaviour, or if you ask them, for example, to moderate their language when on your premises.

Put a copy clearly visible on a noticeboard where it can be seen by parents and visitors. If parents volunteer to help out or you have trainees with you, point it out to them on their first visit and ask them to read it through and take notice of it.

TOP TIP!

On their first visit, give the volunteer or trainee a cup of coffee, a copy of the policy, and direct them to a comfy chair in a quiet place and ask them to take time to read it through. Let them see how important it is.

You could make a child-friendly version of the part where you describe the behaviour you want to see, and place copies of it around the setting, indoors and out. Use it when you notice something good: point to the line that says *we will all look after each other*, and say 'I noticed that Sam and Grace let our new friend, Ellie, join in their game this morning. Well done. I hope you all had a lovely time making friends.' Refer to it if you see unacceptable behaviour: 'Taylor, do you remember that it says here *we share our toys*? Well, that means that if you have all of the dough and someone else wants to play with it, then you should give them some of the dough, as well as keeping some of it for yourself.'

A sample policy

Below is a sample of what your policy could look like when you have completed it.

- Use the notes from the meeting to fill in each of the sections and hand copies to all those involved in the meeting.
- Give them a chance to read through it, mark on it any ideas they have and collect the copies in again.

- Redraft as necessary and then hand out final copies.

- Remember to add the date on which it was finalised and the date when you will review it. It's probably worth looking at it again at the start of each year as it is a reminder to all staff of the culture and atmosphere in which you and your children will be working.

The instructions for you to follow are in *italics*.

The sample wording of the policy is displayed in a bullet list.

These are only ideas to start you thinking. Modify them, or create your own so that your policy fits well into your particular setting.

There is a blank format of this on the website www.pearsoned.co.uk/essentialguides that you can download and modify.

Our Nursery Behaviour Management Policy

What you hope to achieve

At Our Nursery our aim is that all of the children should be able to behave in socially acceptable ways.

Explain what that means in easy-to-follow language

To be socially acceptable we believe that the children at Our Nursery should:

- Treat other children and adults with respect and kindness

- Speak politely to other people

- Have self-confidence and high self-esteem

- Look after the resources and their environment

- Expect to be treated with respect, kindness and tolerance

Explain what you will do to achieve this

To encourage this, the staff at Our Nursery will:

- Provide a positive culture in which children can be nurtured

- Treat all children and adults with respect

- Speak politely to all other people

- Praise children's efforts and achievements as often as they can

- Explain to children what they should have done or said when they get it wrong
- Tell parents about their child's efforts and achievements
- Avoid using critical or sarcastic language
- Maintain the setting, equipment and resources in good order
- Work with parents when a child's behaviour is causing concern
- Work with other professionals to modify a child's behaviour if that is necessary

Explain what you won't accept

At Our Nursery we will not accept the following behaviours from children or adults:

- Use of rude or unkind language
- Hitting, kicking, biting or other such physical responses
- Racist or sexist remarks

Explain what you will do if this is happening

If children behave like this we will:

- Tell the child that it is wrong and explain what they should have done or said [or not said]
- If the behaviour is repeated, the child will be reminded once more as above
- If the behaviour continues we will remove the child from the activity
- We will speak to the parent when the child is collected
- Together with the parent we will try to find out why the child is behaving this way and then treat the situation accordingly

If staff behave like this we will:

- The leader will speak to the member of staff in private as soon as possible
- If it continues …

If parents or visitors behave like this we will:

- The leader will ask the parent to speak to her away from the children or other parents, and will remind her of the nursery policy

Explain any regulations or laws you have to follow

We follow these regulations …

Identify any support systems/people you can call on, when, how, why

We can get help from …

Complaints and compliments

● If you are not happy with the way that you or your child is treated by any member of the staff or another parent at Our Nursery you should …

● If you are pleased with the way that your child's behaviour has been managed by our staff you should …

A children's version of the behaviour policy

Chapter 9 includes ideas for involving the children in creating this. There is a format for this on the website www.pearsoned.co.uk/essentialguides.

Here are a few sample policies.

At Our Nursery

We will be kind to each other

We will share with each other

We will help each other

We will walk when we are indoors

We will speak quietly when we are indoors

… so that everyone can be happy here

At Our Nursery

Be good

Be kind

Be friendly

Be careful

Be polite

… and have a great time

Appendix 2
PROFESSIONAL CODE OF CONDUCT

It is up to the adults who have responsibility for the children to set a good example. This applies particularly to behaviour. Children imitate what they see happening around them, whether you intend them to see it or not. They learn how to behave by watching adults and copying what they see, in the assumption that this is what is expected of them. Having an agreed Code of Conduct for staff is a way of setting the standard of behaviour in your workplace. The discussion about what is to be included in the Code can be a useful management tool, helping to focus everyone's attention on their own behaviour.

Even if your setting doesn't have a formal Code of Conduct it is important that you think about your own behaviour. You could use the ideas here as you think about how your behaviour might be influencing the way that your children are behaving.

Each chapter of this book contains a discussion of some aspect of staff conduct within the same frame of reference as the discussions about the children's developing behaviour. To create your own Code of Conduct you could take each of these in turn, discuss its implications and its application, arriving at an agreed statement, as the following headings show.

What is socially acceptable

We will keep to the nursery/school routines so that the whole staff team can work together for the benefit of the children.

What is morally acceptable

We will treat all people fairly.

Respecting other people, their person, their culture and their property

We will maintain confidentiality.

Developing the ability to forge and maintain relationships

We will work with our colleagues in ways that will foster professional growth and development.

Developing self-control and emotional balance

We will remain calm and in control of our own emotions.

Developing self-respect and a sense of personal pride

We will act, speak and behave as professionals at all times to the children, the parents, our colleagues and other professionals.

Behaving so that learning can take place

We will carry out our duties responsibly.

Having a positive outlook on life

We will always put the children's needs first, no matter how we are feeling.

We will create an atmosphere that allows enjoyment and fun.

Being ready to learn

We will have high expectations of all of the children, encouraging them to achieve their best, praising their efforts and achievements.

These agreed statements could be your Code of Conduct. If you are writing it up as a formal Code, which might be displayed on a noticeboard, omit the headings in bold print. Simply list your own agreed statements.

Alternatively, you could group these statements under three headings:

1. We will act professionally at all times.
2. We will demonstrate high standards of behaviour.

3. We will show respect for all people.

You can now set out your own specific statements under these banner headlines.

We will act professionally at all times

- We will speak to children politely, calmly and with respect.
- We will speak to parents, visitors and colleagues politely, calmly and with respect.
- We will maintain confidentiality.
- We will carry out our duties responsibly and according to agreed systems.
- We will keep our records up to date and in good order.
- We will maintain a professional appearance.

We will demonstrate high standards of behaviour

- We will remain calm at all times.
- We will be honest and trustworthy.
- We will use appropriate language.

We will show respect for all people

- We will treat everyone equally.
- We will support our colleagues.
- We will act respectfully towards other professionals.
- We will never discriminate against other people.

There are samples of these codes on the website www.pearsoned.co.uk/essential guides that you can modify and download.

References and additional reading

Used throughout the book

DfES (2007) *The Early Years Foundation Stage. Setting the Standards for Learning, Development and Care for Children from Birth to Five*, Nottingham: DfES. Folder contains the books:

● Statutory Framework for the Early Years Foundation Stage.

● Practice Guidance for the Early Years Foundation Stage.

www.teachernet.gov.uk/publications

www.dcsf.gov.uk/everychildmatters

Chapter 1

Abbott, L. and Langston A. (eds) (2005) *Birth to Three Matters. Supporting the Framework of Effective Practice,* Maidenhead: Open University Press.

Cousins, L. and Jennings, J. (2003) *The Positive Behaviour Handbook. The Complete Guide to Promoting Positive Behaviour in Your School,* London: pfp publishing.

Edgington, M. (2005) *The Foundation Stage Teacher in Action. Teaching 3, 4 and 5 Year Olds,* London: Paul Chapman.

Eisenberg A., Murkoff, H.E. and Hathaway S.E. (1996) *What to Expect. The Toddler Years,* London: Simon & Schuster.

Jenner, S. (1999) *The Parent/Child Game. The Proven Key to a Happier Family,* London: Bloomsbury.

Miller, L. (1992) *Understanding Your 4 Year Old,* London: Rosendale Press.

Schaffer, H.R. (2004) *Introducing Child Psychology,* Oxford: Blackwell.

Chapter 2

Bee, H. (1989, 5th edn) *The Developing Child,* New York: Harper & Row.

Blakemore, S-J., and Frith, U. (2005) *The Learning Brain. Lessons for Education*, Oxford: Blackwell.

Davenport, G.C. (1994, 2nd edn) *An Introduction to Child Development,* London: Collins Educational.

Evans, D. (2001) *Emotion. A Very Short Introduction,* Oxford: Oxford University Press.

Layard, R. and Dunn, J. (2009) *A Good Childhood. Searching for Values in a Competitive Age*, London: Penguin.

Licht, B., Simoni, H. and Perrig-Chiello, P. (2008) 'Conflict between peers in infancy and toddler age: What do they fight about?', *Early Years, An International Journal of Research and Development,* 28, 3, October 2008, 235–249.

Schaffer, H.R. (2004) *Introducing Child Psychology,* Oxford: Blackwell.

Smith, P., Cowie, H. and Black, M. (2003, 4th edn) *Understanding Children's Development,* Oxford: Blackwell.

Turiel, E. (1998, 5th edn) 'The development of morality', in W. Damon and N. Eisenberg (eds), *Handbook of Child Psychology: Vol. 3. Social, Emotional and Personal*, New York: Wiley, 863–892.

Zahn-Waxler, C. and Radke-Yarrow, M. (1982) 'The development of altruism: Alternative research strategies', in N. Eisenberg (ed.), *The Development of Pro-social Behaviour*, New York: Academic Press, cited in Smith et al. (2003).

Chapter 3

Bartsch, K. and Wellman, H.M. (1995) *Children Talk About the Mind*, Oxford: Oxford University Press.

Blakemore, S.J. and Frith, U. (2005) *The Learning Brain. Lessons for Education*, Oxford: Blackwell.

Brown, B. (2002) *Unlearning Discrimination in the Early Years*, Stoke on Trent: Trentham Books.

Carter, R. (2003) *Mapping the Mind,* London: Phoenix.

Fancourt, R. (2000) *Brainy Babies,* London: Penguin.

Flavell, J.H. (2002) 'Development of children's knowledge about the mental world', in W.W. Hartup and R.K. Silbereisen (eds), *Growing Points in Developmental Science*, Hove: Psychology Press.

Gerhardt, S. (2004) *Why Love Matters. How Affection Shapes a Baby's Brain,* Hove: Brunner-Routledge.

Martin, P. (2006) *Making People Happy. The Nature of Happiness and its Origins in Childhood,* London: Harper Perennial.

McKee, D. (2007) *Elmer*, London: Andersen Press.

O'Shea, M. (2005) *The Brain. A Very Short Introduction*, Oxford: Oxford University Press.

Schaffer, H.R. (2004) *Introducing Child Psychology,* Oxford: Blackwell.

Severe, S. (2000) *How to Behave so Your Children Will, Too.* London: Vermilion.

Smith, P., Cowie, H. and Black, M. (2003, 4th edn) *Understanding Children's Development,* Oxford: Blackwell Publishing.

Chapter 4

Ainsworth, M., Blehar, M., Waters, E. and Wall, S. (1978) *Patterns of Attachment. A Psychological Study of the Strange Situation*, Hillsdale, NJ: Lawrence Erlbaum Associates.

Bowlby, J. (1969) *Attachment and Loss: Vol 1. Attachment*, New York: Basic Books.

Edgington, M. (2005) *The Foundation Stage Teacher in Action. Teaching 3, 4 and 5 Year Olds,* London: Paul Chapman.

Flanagan, C. (2008) *Applying Psychology to Early Child Development*, London: Hodder Education.

Gordon, R. (1996) *The Primary Behaviour File*, London: pfp publishing.

Herschkowitz, N. and Herschkowitz, E.C. (2002) *A Good Start in Life. Understanding Your Child's Brain and Behaviour,* Washington, DC: Joseph Henry Press.

Miller, L. (1992) *Understanding Your 4 Year Old,* London: Rosendale Press.

Mukherji, P. (2001) *Understanding Children's Challenging Behaviour,* Cheltenham: Nelson Thornes.

Schaffer, H.R. (2004) *Introducing Child Psychology,* Oxford: Blackwell Publishing.

Smith, P., Cowie, H. and Black, M. (2003, 4th edn) *Understanding Children's Development,* Oxford: Blackwell.

Sroufe, L.A. (1989) Talk at City University of New York Graduate Center, 10 February, cited in Karen, R. (1998) *Becoming Attached. First Relationships and How They Shape our Capacity to Love*, New York: Oxford University Press.

Chapter 5

Carter, R. (2003) *Mapping the Mind,* London: Phoenix.

Connellan, T., Baron-Cohen, S., Wheelwright, S., Ba'tki, A. and Ahluwalia, J. (2001) 'Sex differences in human neonatal social perception', *Infant Behaviour and Development*, 23, 113–118.

Fancourt, R. (2000) *Brainy Babies,* London: Penguin.

Gerhardt, S. (2004) *Why Love Matters. How Affection Shapes a Baby's Brain,* Hove: Brunner-Routledge.

Hall, J.A. (1978) 'Gender effects in decoding nonverbal cues', *Psychological Bulletin,* 85, 845–858.

Hammond, C. (2005) *Emotional Rollercoaster. A Journey through the Science of Feelings*, London: Fourth Estate.

Happe, F. (1995) 'The role of age and verbal ability in the theory of mind task performance of subjects with autism', *Child Development*, 66, 843–855.

Morain, G.G. (1986) 'Kinesics and Cross-cultural Understanding', in J.M. Valdes, (ed.), *Culture Bound: Bridging the Gap in Language Teaching,* Cambridge: Cambridge University Press.

Peake, T.H. and Egli, D. (1982) 'The language of feelings', *Journal of Contemporary Psychotherapy*, 13, 2, 162–174.

Schaffer, H.R. (2004) *Introducing Child Psychology,* Oxford: Blackwell.

Smith, P., Cowie, H. and Black, M. (2003, 4th edn) *Understanding Children's Development,* Oxford: Blackwell.

Chapter 6

Coopersmith, S. (1967) *The Antecedents of Self-esteem,* San Francisco, CA: W.H. Freeman (cited in Schaffer, 2004, p 311).

Corrie, C. (2003) *Becoming Emotionally Intelligent,* Stafford: Network Educational Press.

Cousins, L. and Jennings, J. (2003) *The Positive Behaviour Handbook. The Complete Guide to Promoting Positive Behaviour in your School*, London: pfp publishing.

Degotardi, S. and Davis, B. (2008) 'Understanding infants: Characteristics of early childhood practitioners' interpretations of infants and their behaviours', *Early Years, An International Journal of Research and Development*, 28, 3, 221–234.

Hughes D. (2006) *Building the Bonds of Attachment,* Northvale, NJ: Jason Aronson.

Jenner, S. (1999) *The Parent/Child Game. The Proven Key to a Happier Family*, London: Bloomsbury.

Lewis, M. and Brooks-Gunn, J. (1979) *Social Cognition and the Acquisition of Self,* New York: Plenum Press.

Livesley, W.J. and Bromley, D.B. (1973) *Person Perception in Children and Adolescents*, London: Wiley.

McKee, (1996, re-issued 2002) *Not Now, Bernard*, London: Red Fox.

Schaffer, H.R. (2004) *Introducing Child Psychology,* Oxford: Blackwell.

Smith, P., Cowie, H. and Black, M. (2003, 4th edn) *Understanding Children's Development,* Oxford: Blackwell.

Sunderland, M. (2003) *Helping Children with Low Self-esteem,* Bicester: Speechmark Publishing.

Chapter 7

Blakemore, S-J. and Frith, U. (2005) *The Learning Brain. Lessons for Education*, Oxford: Blackwell.

Brierley, J. (1994, 2nd edn) *Give Me a Child Until he is Seven*. Lewes: Falmer Press.

Carter, R. (2003) *Mapping the Mind,* London: Phoenix.

Donaldson, M (1989) *Children's Minds,* London: Fontana Press.

Fisher, R. (1995) *Teaching Children to Think*, Cheltenham: Stanley Thornes.

Nutbrown, C. (2006, 3rd edn) *Threads of Thinking. Young Children Learning and the Role of Early Education,* London: Sage.

O'Shea, M. (2005) *The Brain. A Very Short Introduction*, Oxford: Oxford University Press

Smith, P., Cowie, H. and Black, M. (2003, 4th edn) *Understanding Children's Development,* Oxford: Blackwell Publishing.

Chapter 8

Anning, A. (1991) *The First Years at School*, Buckingham: Open University Press.

Athey, C. (2007, 2nd edn) *Extending Thought in Young Children. A Parent–Teacher Approach,* London: Paul Chapman.

Carter, R. (2003) *Mapping the Mind,* London: Phoenix.

Fisher, R. (ed.) (1987) *Problem Solving in Primary Schools,* Oxford: Basil Blackwell.

Jenner, S. (1999) *The Parent/Child Game. The Proven Key to a Happier Family,* London: Bloomsbury.

Mukherji, P. (2001) *Understanding Children's Challenging Behaviour,* Cheltenham: Nelson Thornes.

Urwin, C. and Hood-Williams, J. (eds) (1988) *Selected Papers of Margaret Lowenfeld,* London: Free Association Books.

Chapter 9

Fisher, R. (1995) *Teaching Children to Think*, Cheltenham: Stanley Thornes.

Hutchins, P. (1989) *The Doorbell Rang*, New York: William Morrow.

Layard, R. and Dunn, J. (2009) *A Good Childhood. Searching for Values in a Competitive Age,* London: Penguin.

Martin, P. (2006) *Making People Happy. The Nature of Happiness and its Origins in Childhood*, London: Harper Perennial.

Moon, N. (2007) *Something Special,* London: Orchard Books.

Pfister, M. (1992) *The Rainbow Fish*, New York: North South Books.

Conclusion

Gerhardt, S. (2004) *Why Love Matters. How Affection Shapes a Baby's Brain,* Hove: Brunner-Routledge.

Index

The Essential Guides Series

Practical skills for teachers

The Essential Guides series offers a wealth of practical support, inspiration and guidance for NQTs and more experienced teachers ready to implement into their classroom. The books provide practical advice and tips on the core aspects of teaching and everyday classroom issues, such as planning, assessment, behaviour and ICT. The Essential Guides are invaluable resources that will help teachers to successfully navigate the challenges of the profession.

The Essential Guide to
Successful School Trips
John Trant

© 2010 paperback
ISBN 978-1-4082-0447-4

The Essential Guide to
Using ICT Creatively in the Primary Classroom
Steve Woods

© 2010 paperback
ISBN 978-1-4082-2497-7

The Essential Guide to
Secondary Teaching
Susan Davies

© 2010 paperback
ISBN 978-1-4082-2452-6

The Essential Guide to
Classroom Assessment
Paul Dix

© 2010 paperback
ISBN 978-1-4082-3025-1

The Essential Guide to
Taking Care of Behaviour
(second edition)
Paul Dix

© 2010 paperback
ISBN 978-1-4082-2554-7

The Essential Guide to
Teaching 14-19 Diplomas
Lynn Senior

© 2010 paperback
ISBN 978-1-4082-2549-3

The Essential Guide to
Understanding Special Educational Needs
Jenny Thompson

© 2010 paperback
ISBN 978-1-4082-2500-4

Longman
is an imprint of

PEARSON

Practical skills for teachers

RICHMOND UPON THAMES COLLEGE LIBRARY